From Cur: Ketch:

the Story of Minehead's Quay Town

Previously published works by the Genge Press:

The Man who was Cyrano: a Life of Edmond Rostand, Creator of 'Cyrano de Bergerac' by Sue Lloyd (USA: UP, 2003;UK: GP, 2007)

Poems, by Brigid Somerset, 2003

The Two Pierrots or The White Supper, a verse translation of Edmond Rostand's play, *Les Deux Pierrots,* by Thom Christoph, 2007

The Anarchist Geographer: an Introduction to the Life of Peter Kropotkin, by Brian Gilman, 2007

Chantecler, by Edmond Rostand, introduced and annotated by Sue Lloyd, 2010

All titles are in print and available on application to the Genge Press

In Preparation:

Sacred and Profane Love: Two Plays by Edmond Rostand: The Woman of Samaria, translated by Philippa Gerry and Sue Lloyd; *Don Juan's Final Night,* translated by Sonia Yates and Sue Lloyd

From Curragh to Ketch: the Story of Minehead's Quay Town

by

John Gilman and Sue Lloyd

John Gilman

and Sue Lloyd,

Genge Press

4

Genge Press, 45 Quay Street, Minehead TA24 5UL
www.gengepress.co.uk

© John Gilman & Sue Lloyd 2012

A CIP Record for this book is available from the British Library

ISBN 978 0 9549043 5 7

Cover photograph: detail from a water colour painting in the
John Gilman collection, dated around 1820s

Printed by First Design and Print, Porlock
on FSC Mixed Credit paper.

Contents

6

Illustrations

Except where otherwise acknowledged, all photographs are from the Escott and Gilman collections, with end-of-chapter motifs drawn by John Gilman. Kevin Escott and John Gilman record their grateful thanks to the photographers and artists who have contributed to these important historical records.

Our thanks for sharing individual illustrations go to Oliver Davies for plate 8; to Diana Bruford for 12 and 13b; to John Rawle for 16c and 29; to Edna Caley for 26b, to Pat Turner for 27 and 32 and to Noreen Matthews for 31(a) and 31(b). The authors are also grateful to everyone who shared their photographs with us, even though we could not use them all.

Introduction

We have called this book a 'Story' because it is not intended to be an exhaustive history — there are already several good histories of Minehead available — but because it is intended to give a flavour of how our predecessors in Quay Town lived and worked up until the end of the Second World War. The harbour was the main focus of Quay Town, so we have also described the kind of vessels that used the harbour and what they were used for. For the more recent chapters we have been able to draw on the actual memories of former and present inhabitants.

The authors

John Gilman, writer, artist and poet, grew up in Minehead and attended the Grammar School here. National service in the Royal Navy followed by years in ships out of Avonmouth confirmed his already strong interest in the sea and its vessels. After reading history at university, he followed a career in teaching. Now he writes novels and history books with a West Somerset focus, of which *The Girl on the Beach* and *Exmoor's Maritime Heritage* are probably the best known. He is also well known for his ship models. John has contributed to post-graduate research into maritime history, especially as regards Bristol Channel shipping, and has written many papers and articles on this subject. For this book, he has also drawn on his comprehensive collection of photographs of local ports, begun in 1947, and on conversations with well-known coastal seamen such as Captain Philip Stanley Rawle ('Old Stan') and Captain Hugh Shaw.

Now a resident of Quay Street, Sue Lloyd's passion for local history began at the age of ten when she researched the history of her home town, Keynsham. After a career as an editor with publishers such as Longman, Penguin and OUP, she set up the Genge Press in 2003, mainly to publish works by and about the French dramatist Edmond Rostand. Since living in Quay Town she has enjoyed meeting and corresponding with present and former residents who have helped her form a picture, however incomplete, of Quay Town over the ages.

JG and SL, Minehead 2012

8

Acknowledgements

The authors are indebted to many Quay-Town residents past and present for their insights into daily life over the years. Many people have contributed to this book, either directly or indirectly. We owe a particular gratitude to Kevin Escott, former Secretary of the RNLI, who has been generous in sharing his knowledge and large collection of photographs, some of which illustrate this book.

John Rawle, son of Frank Rawle, has been a diligent corespondent and provided photographs and documents; his lively anecdotes have enriched the later chapters. His sister Pat Turner, and Leslie Rawle's daughter, Noreen Matthews, have also shared photographs and recollections with us. Past and present neighbours in Quay Town, including the late Ted Slade and David Medland; Tilla Brading, Marcus & David James, John Malin, Jane Pretty, David Selley, Phil Thresher and especially Diana Bruford have been very helpful with documents, photographs, recollections and other useful information.

Other Minehead friends and acquaintances too numerous to name have contributed to this book. Special thanks to Josephine Lawrence for memories of her father J.S.G. Lawrence, and to Edna Caley for sharing much information, especially about her great-uncle John Etherden. Eileen Ann Moore and Jim Parham investigated the singers of Quay Street, Captain Vickery and Captain Lewis, and persuaded Tom and Barbara Brown to sing some of their songs at an Acorn Folk Club evening in the *Old Ship Aground*. Alison Andrew has been generous in sharing her work on Quay Town censuses and her research into the Webber family, one of whom lived in Sue's present house in Quay Street as a boy.

Fellow members of the Minehead Conservation Society have been very supportive, especially Caroline Giddens, a life-long Minehead resident, and Oliver Davies, who, with the authors, curated the Conservation Society's exhibition in 2010: *Quay Town and the Harbour*, which provided many useful contacts and much material for this book.

Chapter One: The Origins of Minehead as a Port

To understand the origins of Minehead as a port it is helpful to go back to the founding of the so-called 'Western Seaways', used by the tribal traders and voyagers of the Bronze Age and before. As Professor Bowen has amply demonstrated in his *Britain and the Western Seaways* (1972), these were major sea routes that developed from earliest times down to the Celts, the raids of the Vikings and the later medieval traders. It is often hard to comprehend that at least three thousand years ago ocean-going vessels were capable of making lengthy voyages with reasonable safety all down the western side of the European mainland including the thousands of inlets and offshore islands. Intrepid seafarers such as the Veneti of Britanny set up regular patterns of trade and communication along the coastal ribbon from Gibraltar to Iceland including all the major channels, straits and ria estuaries of the Atlantic coast.

The key to this remarkable ongoing venture in maritime trade lay in the vessels of the day. Equally remarkable is the fact that many have survived in one form or another. The curragh, still found in Ireland, is the direct descendant of the vessel made of hide stretched over a wicker frame that made this early pattern possible. There is no doubt that such curraghs regularly crossed the Atlantic via Iceland and Greenland and formed the major means of transport for every domestic and trade product up and down the Western European coast from Neolithic times. The seamanship of the Celts and their forebears in these islands was of the highest quality. We know that curraghs of up to sixty feet with a beam of up to fifteen feet were at home in all conditions and weathers of the Atlantic Ocean and the Irish Sea.

Nevertheless, the Celts did not rely totally on this type of vessel and also employed a planked variety for shorter coastal and estuary work. Recently the remains of one of these planked vessels was found off Salcombe, on the South Devon coast. Described as a bulk carrier, she was carrying tin and copper ingots and measured some forty feet in length. Dating from over three thousand years ago, this boat indicates that the tin and copper trade was established at the time and there were seamen to transport its products.

The Celtic seafarer's knowledge of local seaways was likely to be as detailed as his knowledge of the locality, its fields, hills and footpaths. Local coastal navigation has always been a feature of this region, some passages forming part of longer ones which extended southwards across to the continent and northwards into Wales. Overland routes were sometimes combined with these. For example, it was often the practice in Celtic times to move valuable cargoes across the South-West peninsula rather than brave winter seas off the Lizard. Ancient trackways show that it was possible to land a cargo in the Exe estuary, follow the river valleys of the Exe and Barle, cross over the Brendon ridge and fork either right for Watchet or left for Minehead via the Roadwater or Avill valleys. The passage onwards from Minehead was traditionally to Aberthaw in South Wales, known as the Port of the Vale of Glamorgan.

An important factor in choosing a harbour is the landscape itself. Natural harbours are rare along the ironbound, hog-backed cliff faces that Exmoor presents to the sea. Places where vessels could shelter, beach or ride at anchor in safety were rare, so a 'haven' harbour was of great value. Formed naturally behind the shingle ridges where a local stream had run parallel to the sea for a while before pushing a way through, these shallow basins were ideal in providing shelter from the sea and a safe landfall. They occurred naturally at Porlock Weir, Porlock Marsh, Dunster Beach and Carhampton as well as formerly at Minehead. It was not too difficult to establish and maintain the entrances of these natural features to secure a good permanent harbour. Porlock Weir is perhaps the best extant example of this, where the entrance was finally made good in stone in the fifteenth century and the little harbour has remained much the same ever since. This particular 'haven' was formed by the Worthy Water before its course was altered in the seventeenth century during a great storm. Dunster's 'haven', or Hawn as it came to be known, was in use through the Saxon period and well into the Norman era under the Norman lords of Dunster.

Minehead's Bratton Water originally ran down the site of the present Avenue and turned westwards inside the shingle ridge to form a 'haven' before exiting into the sea at a point close to the bottom of Blenheim Road. This was the position of the earliest harbour. In living memory, the remains of the shingle ridge were merged with the sea defences. The ground level within the old basin is still lower than the Promenade, as is clearly visible inside the Jubilee Gardens grounds (now a Crazy Golf course). In the eighteenth-century 'The Haven' became known as a place where old vessels were laid up. The former Beachhaven Hotel perhaps recalls this use. Closer to North Hill the water increases in depth as the gently shelving beach of the bay comes up against the cliffs. This was the reason for siting the present harbour, built by 1616, at that end of the beach.

The local fisherfolk would have known the foreshore well. Like ancient field names, seamarks and the names of the local banks and flats would have been known and there is evidence that the foreshore was extensively worked, modified and used for trapping and catching fish. The seamarks both above and below Minehead are very old and the ridges and banks have not shifted much over the centuries. Sprat Ridge and Bull Ridge to the east, close to Ker Moor, are features of the coast that would have been there from the earliest days of settlement.

The sites chosen for harbours were not only natural but fitted into the larger patterns of trade already mentioned. They were strategic, defensible, and answered local needs. In Minehead's case the 'haven' was sheltered from the prevailing westerlies and indeed, all the major sources of gales except the east. All through her history it has only been the easterlies that were feared locally. Acting as a look-out and a navigational base point, North Hill not only provided the necessary strategic high ground but tied the communities of hill and haven together in a way that remains true in Minehead today. In addition, the Bratton Water flowed through a sheltered valley entirely hidden from the sea. This is a pattern to be found in many Celtic-based settlements where domestic agriculture, farming and fishing were allied with trade and wider communication. It is very likely that Minehead owes its origins to the first farmers and seafarers of the Middle Bronze Age, the period around 1500-1,000 BC, with their liking for high ground but their realisation that the hidden south-facing sheltered valleys could provide surpluses for trade. Groups of roundhouses and walled enclosures may well have existed set into the hill and lower down on the sheltered side below the spring line. The sites of Lower Moor Farm and Shute Farm answer all these points, as do the Mynes of North Hill.

This region of coast escaped the major upheavals of the Roman occupation and apart from the obvious benefits of a stable national administration, was little disturbed by the occasional comings and goings of military personnel and the few merchant travellers. The tribal boundaries had not been disturbed and the neighbouring tribes, the Durotriges and the Dobunni beyond the River Parret, who had been more extensively Romanised, did not impinge upon the ancient and accepted freedoms enjoyed along the coast and up the various navigable rivers. Only with the final withdrawal of the Romans in 410 did the region find itself with the responsibility of both national and tribal security.

Just along the coast at Carhampton a Celtic monastery was set up, probably by St Carantoc or one of his followers in the late sixth century. As this section of coast was not swamped by the Saxons until the 680s, there was ample time for Christianity to spread into the region and become established well before Augustinian Christianity swept in with the Saxons, with the Synod of Whitby in 664 marking the great national change as Celtic Christianity was submerged in favour of obedience to the Pope.

The end of the 680s also marked the end of the so-called 'Age of the Saints' in which idiosyncratic and charismatic personalities such as Decuman, Petroc, Dubricius and Cadoc travelled widely along the western seaways bringing the gospel and an austere way of life in community that encouraged a deep spiritual appreciation of life and the wider world. Following this, the Augustinian church organised itself more on urban lines and the multitude of isolated chapels and monastic communities were re-arranged, often re-dedicated and re-built.

By the first quarter of the eighth century most of the best valley sites ended up in Saxon hands as did the administration and organisation of trade and communications. Dunster, guarding the Avill hinterland and the route to the south, was soon in Saxon hands with its port at the Hawn. Minehead was certainly recognised for its importance as it too guarded a valley entrance to the west and an important route overland across Hopcott Hill, Hooey Cross and the river route to the Exe estuary. One of the clues that we are at a crossroads of social control is the loss at this time of Minehead's Celtic church dedication and the re-establishment of the church under Augustinian rule. It was the practice at the time to remove the Celtic church altogether and make a fresh start on a new site. At Minehead, as elsewhere, this was resisted. There was a Celtic cell or small oratory on the site of St Michael's Church. It was sited, as prescribed, on a distinct bearing within the north aisle and north wall of the present church. The church was then enlarged, overlying the original building entirely, and the original naming or dedication was obliterated.

Church and harbour are strongly linked in the case of Minehead and probably since the original saint climbed up from the beach and laid out the plan. The plan for all the early Celtic Christian settlements followed some quite distinct pointers. There must be a hill or preferably an outcrop of rock. This must be approached by a steep or winding path and the site must have a spring. At St Michael's there is a raised rocky plateau set above an outcrop presently clad in a wall, some twenty feet above the road at the top of Church Steps. To the east there lies the spring in the field opposite the churchyard where the spring-line brings a supply of good water flowing towards the old yard at the back of Shute Farm. (On a dry summer's day the shape of the arms of this watercourse can still be clearly seen etched in brighter green on the yellowing grass.) We have the rock, the spring and the steep ascent. Finally we have the dimensions of the oratory, lying along the lines as clear today as they were to the original founder who recognised and planned this holy site.

Passing from the church down to the the working part of the old haven harbour was an ancient track or pathway. Various stories link the church with the harbour. One has it that the church provided a light to aid navigation; in the later church of the fifteenth century this light was kept in the rood stairwell. Any vessel would have to be well into the bay to be able to see a light in that position, so the church light was probably just a marker to indicate that Minehead had been passed and it was safe to drop back into the shelter of the hill. The traditional anchorage is just below the harbour at White Mark, a mark on the cliff kept painted white to this day, showing where it is safe for a boat to wait for the tide to come in.

By the time of the Saxons inshore fishing would have been well established. Weirs were built, too, right across the bay. Rents were payable to the lords of the manor at Dunster, who owned the whole foreshore. The remains of these angular weirs with ancient names such as Martin's Weir, are easy to see at low tide. The use of nets strung out from posts is also very old; the remains of the posts can be found running out into the bay at low water. In the oldest records they are referred to as *les stackes in mari* or stakes in the sea, which is what they were. One line of poles on Minehead beach is still in occasional use.

Viking raids from the sea started in earnest in the 9th century. Minehead was not important enough to interest the invaders, but at Carhampton, as the Anglo-Saxon Chronicle records, King Egbert, King of Wessex, fought against twenty-five ships' companies of invading 'Danes' in 836 and lost the day. In 843, his son, King Aethelwulf, with the local levies, met another huge host of sea pirates on the foreshore close to Ker Moor at Carhampton and after a hard day, retired from the fight with great loss of life. The so-called 'Danes' were really a vast collection of mercenaries and pirates from many nations around the Baltic, Danish and Friesian coasts. They were out for what they could get by conquest, booty or theft in unstable times. Roving in bands of up to two thousand at a time, they lived off the land and set up camp wherever they might find sufficient reward. Their custom of looting and burning settlements meant they could extort payment to leave areas alone; this brought great hardship to the local ports and villages.

However, the speed and capacity of the Viking longships inspired new designs for larger traders and deep-sea vessels, once peace was established again. Wooden craft smaller and broader than the Viking warships were developed with a greater depth in hold. These plied up and down the coast with cattle and sheep, domestic goods and timber, stone or wool on a daily basis. Markets were used on both sides of the Channel and it was normal for a Minehead trader to be as well-known in the Welsh ports and in Ireland as in his home port.

Whereas the Celts had generations to acclimatise to the slow inroads of the Saxons, the Normans were building their motte and bailey castles everywhere within years of their arrival. Dunster Castle and its Lords soon dominated the region. The sea had been the Normans' pathway to conquest and it was to the sea that the Normans looked for their already-established trading patterns. Even their stone came from Normandy in tough little sailing coasters, so Dunster Hawn was dredged and lengthened. There are references to it as a port in early papers and it certainly outshone the more primitive 'haven' at Carhampton which soon decayed and dropped out of use.

Minehead came under the jurisdiction of Dunster Castle and continued in use as a fishing and trading centre but its harbour was not, initially, as important as Dunster's, which was nearer to the castle. The entrance to Minehead haven had to be kept at a good depth to accommodate the gradual increase in tonnage. That this need was recognised is seen in the very earliest records we have, where it was prohibited for anyone to throw stones into the haven thus contributing to the loss of working depth. The next stage of development would have been the construction of an arm, probably made of protruding timber baulks, set to prevent longshore drift from obstructing the harbour entrance. This was the first jetty or working construction beyond the shingle and extending on to the beach. Its site would have been roughly opposite where the modern Red Lion, now aptly renamed the Quay Inn, was sited. Quay Lane also owes its name to its position by the wharfs of the ancient harbour.

Local craft were adapted to landing on open beaches and discharging their cargoes over the side but the haven was maintained as well, as it provided more shelter than an open harbour could do. Dunster had a much larger 'haven' harbour as the Avill River ran eastwards alongside the shingle for a considerable distance before punching through to the sea, just to the west of the present storm drain. But all the local harbours shared a problem: they were subject to longshore drift from the west across their entrances which as a result were prone to becoming clogged with beach stones, especially during spring tides, thus decreasing the working depth of the harbour. In the Middle Ages, the Luttrells apparently left a percentage of the tolls due to them from trading to the townspeople of Minehead, to pay for keeping the entrance clear.

By the end of the fourteenth century, trading from Minehead Haven Harbour was already well-established and even flourishing, as can be seen from the custom dues payable to the Crown. As Dunster Hawn silted up, Minehead harbour increased in importance and prosperity. Around 1421, Lady Catherine Luttrell gave ten shillings towards a 'new juttee' to protect the merchant ships at Minehead. Such ships were already trading to Bristol, South Wales, and, because of the Luttrell connection, to France, where they took local fish and brought back wine for the Lords of the Manor. In 1418, for instance, we have a record of the *Leonard of Donesterre*, under Philip Clapton, sailing to Bordeaux. Another trader, Roger King, used to call at various ports along the coast to collect goods from the scattered Luttrell manors to take to Normandy.

Fish were an important part of the early medieval diet, as the Church decreed that meat should not eaten on Mondays or Wednesdays as well as Fridays. A variety of fish including sprats, herrings, conger eels, ray fish and even the occasional sturgeon were caught off Minehead Bay. When Sir Hugh set off again for the French Wars in 1419, the supplies sent down to his ship included thirteen-and-a-half dozen ling and millwell ('mulvel', i.e. cod), one hundred conger eels and four casks of herrings. Much of this fish would have been salted to preserve it.

Like other places that were not politically important but stood at the crossroads of coastal and agricultural inter-dependency, Minehead now began to develop as a small township, but in three separate parts: Higher Town, Lower or Middle Town, and Quay Town.

Chapter Two: Minehead in Tudor and Early Stuart Times

Seafarer William Donnell, at one hundred or so years of age, was Minehead's oldest resident at the end of the sixteenth century. If one day he sat on the sea wall at the end of Quay Street, gazing out to sea, he would have seen the huge boulders of the New Quay, now nearly completed. It was to be a quay of unsurpassed strength and durability. The boulders, weighing many tons each, had been floated across from Greenaleigh on special rafts, with air-filled casks lashed to each boulder.

If William then turned eastwards he would see, some four hundred paces away, the blackened timbers of the old jetty leaning against a huge bank of shingle. It could not now accommodate even the smallest vessel, even though ships of a hundred tons and more used to discharge their cargo there.

For by the end of the fifteenth century Minehead had become a considerable port. Trade had increased during the reign of Henry VII, and in around 1485 the new Lord of the Manor, Sir Hugh Luttrell, thought it worthwhile to build another small jetty to increase the original harbour's capacity; he enlarged it a few years later. Ships, some owned by Minehead men, arrived here from France, Spain and Portugal. Small square-rigged vessels traded across the Bristol Channel, while others sailed to Ireland, where a considerable trade, especially in livestock and wool, had been established with the West Country over the last two centuries. There was also a brisk trade with Bridgwater in beans, salt, wood, iron and coal, along with wine probably imported from Europe. Ships from Minehead also fished the Channel approaches and the coasts of Ireland for herring, and some were part of a fishing fleet that sailed to Iceland in season for cod.

However, all these vessels were easy prey to the French, Flemish and Spanish privateers who, taking out 'letters of marque' (official permission to capture ships from hostile countries), went cruising the seas to take by force what vessels they could. The division between privateers and pirates was often obscure, as the letters of marque were often from little-known dominions and colonies. All kinds of vessels were used for this quick route to riches, and the inlets in south and south-western Ireland in particular provided ideal bases from which to make sorties. Many honest merchant ships from Devon and Somerset were captured while attempting to trade with the Irish ports of Kinsdale, Youghal and Cork. *Le Sonday*, which was co-owned by William Donnell's own father, George Donnell, had been captured in this way, and the owners had applied to the Crown for a licence to retaliate, as can be seen from the Patent Rolls of 27 November 1495.

Crews began to go armed to defend themselves; some applied for letters of marque or, like George Donnell, a licence to retaliate. The Bristol Channel and the English Channel became the scene of fierce fighting. The State Papers of the time are full of reports of skirmishes between Devon and Somerset ships and the pirates and privateers. Saving one's life often depended on the speed of one's vessel, so swifter ships were built. The hard school of warfare was honing the fine quality of British seamanship that would continue through the generations.

During the reign of Henry VIII, diplomatic tension grew, with the increasing risk of an invasion across the English Channel. The West Country sent several armed vessels to Sandwich in 1539 to serve with the growing naval fleet. Five years later, when the French appeared to be planning a sortie with 300 ships, the *Saviour* and the *Tawdery* from Minehead were among the swift armed vessels that reported to Portsmouth.

Henry took a personal interest in his seamen and their vessels. The tally of armed vessels in each port grew during his reign. The State Papers for 18 June 1513 noted two such vessels from Bridgwater and two from Minehead, including the *Jesus* 'late of Roane'. By 16 May 1543, the Papers note that in Minehead, William Hyll has a ship of 70 tons, fitted with four small cannons; Robert Quirke has a ship of 60 tons burden, and Lady Luttrell owned a ship of 100 tons which was in London at that time. Dennis Marrane's 60-ton ship was in Ireland. Of mariners, '37 named, besides there are 40 not at home'. These were the only ships belonging to Somerset at that time; there were '13 mariners named' at 'Comage [Combwich] pertaining to Brugewater' but no ships listed. However, this list only contained the names of the larger vessels that might be useful to the king in warfare; it did not include the smaller fishing and trading vessels up to about twenty or thirty tons burden.

A list was drawn up at the end of the sixteenth century by William Donnell with two others, Andrew Teague and William Morgan, at George Luttrell's request, to include all the Minehead ships William could remember that used the harbour before 1558. The list comprised twelve ships, twenty 'barques' and one pinnace. Robert Quirke owned a ship and a bark; so did Dennis Gray, Jon Strading and Yn (John) Dowdinge, whose ship was called the *Great Christover*. Other ships were owned by John Langlie, Will Hill, Rich Coale, Thomas Coale, Teage Porter, Will Roberts (the *Blackboy*), Mr Thos Windham (the *Swan*) and Mr Sully (the *Samewell*). There were fourteen barks listed besides those already mentioned. They belonged to Watkin Thomas, Thomas Stephens, Rob Mackinglin, Luke Gaile, Thomas Youde, Pat Fowler, Stephen Cale (who had two), John Smyth, who shared another barque with Will Donnell; Jon Hill, John Butler (the *Maudlin*), Will Gylse (the *Christover)* and Thos. Hiett. Rich Reade owned the only pinnace listed. (Owners' names are given as in the list.) William Donnell's list was of course the recollection of many years and included vessels lost at sea. It does not imply that all the vessels listed were owned by the town at the same time. Some, such as the *Swan* (co-owned with John Luttrell) and the *Tawdery*, are noted in the Bridgwater harbour accounts for this period, which also name the *Saviour*, owned by Richard King and John Wyndham, the *Michael* (William Thomas), the *Ann*, and Thomas Vennicombe and John Kerry's *Martlet*.

After the death of Henry in 1547, however, the young King Edward VI and then Queen Mary neglected the fleet. Maritime trade suffered as a result. The Icelandic fleet was also disbanded. Many young fishermen from ports in the Bristol Channel joined privateers instead for a life of adventure. Several Minehead vessels are mentioned for acts of piracy in the State Papers of these times. The vessels belonging to the Hill family were notorious, featuring in a number of skirmishes, some in favour with the state, and some decidedly not.

So Minehead, which had thrived during the reign of Henry VIII, now began to suffer badly. Many Minehead fishermen were away manning the larger, swifter ships, engaged in piracy instead of trade. By the time Elizabeth I came to the throne in 1558, it has been estimated that just 50,000 tons of lawfully-engaged shipping remained in all the kingdom.

'It is the secret, determined policy of Spain to destroy the English fleet, Pilots, Masters and Sailors by means of the Inquisition' say the notes of the Privy Council early in Elizabeth's reign. British sea-going communities already felt great hatred for the Spanish as a result of the stories of English sailors taken to Spanish ports and handed over to the Spanish Inquisition on the pretext that they were pirates.

There were now just seven Revenue vessels in the service of the Crown, the largest being 120 tons. These, with eight merchant brigs adapted for fighting, were the only vessels left to prevent piratical activities, defend our coasts and safely convoy the merchant fleets. Losses were heavy and Minehead was deprived of most of her fleet.

At the accession of Queen Elizabeth, Bridgwater and Minehead were the only ports on the 'Severn Sea' apart from Bristol to have port and customs officials. But although Minehead in King Henry VIII's time had harboured more and larger vessels than Bridgwater, now it attracted fewer large ships and did not even have a Customs House of its own. Successive local deputies to the Customs Officer at Bridgwater, namely Robert Quirke, Thomas Pearce and William Beaumont, had had to hire a suitable house in Minehead for 6s.8d a year at their own expense. And although earlier in the sixteenth century, merchant and ship-owners had often left money for the upkeep of the harbour in their wills, as did Thomas Braye in 1513, Robert Burke in 1523 and Thomas Cole in 1526, and although the harbour had been maintained at a yearly charge of £50 a year 'time out of mind', the fact was that the port was decaying rapidly.

It was not simply that wars and piracy had reduced trade and therefore income. The main problem was that the creek that served as a harbour was getting so obstructed by the bank of pebbles (the 'parocke') that had built up at its mouth due to longshore drift, that only small ships trading in small amounts of salt, wine, coal, wood and victuals could now berth there. Efforts had been made to wash out the pebbles by building a weir pool, probably on the site of the present green opposite the public house now known as the Quay Inn (formerly the Red Lion). The idea was that this pool would fill up at high tide and by means of sluices wash away the pebble bank as the tide fell. But even this did not clear the obstruction. The prosperity of the whole town was being affected, and so Minehead traders and ship-owners decided that they would do better to seek independence from the Manor of Dunster and rely on their own efforts.

A petition was therefore sent to Queen Elizabeth in the first year of her reign to secure a charter for the town and port of Minehead to become a free borough, governing itself. The petitioners claimed that although £50 a year had been spent on the upkeep of the harbour, the recent wars had destroyed so much trade that there was now not enough income to keep it in good condition. As a result, the harbour was now almost unusable, to the great detriment of its hinterland in Somerset and as far as Devon and even Cornwall, as the previous trade in cattle and sheep, wool, cloth, butter, stone (limestone), coal and fish could not be carried on safely. Nor could ships passing up or down the Channel take shelter there. What is more, there was great loss of income to the Crown through the loss of import dues. They therefore humbly requested that Minehead become an independent borough, governing itself by means of a Portreeve and Burgesses.

The Queen's Council, after conferring with the Lord of the Manor, Thomas Luttrell, accepted that inland trade had suffered, and agreed that repairing the harbour was urgent. The Council doubtless also took into account the likely loss in income to the Privy Purse from port dues and customs duties. The Charter was granted the same year, 1559. Minehead would now be governed by a Portreeve and twelve burgesses, who together would appoint a steward. The first Portreeve was John Dodinge (Dowding), owner of the *Great Christopher*, while the burgesses included other prominent mariners and ship owners such as Robert Quirke, John Kerry (the master of Vice Admiral Thomas Wyndham's ship), and William Donnell. Perhaps remembering how his own father's ship had been captured by privateers, the latter doubtless hoped for a clear harbour, a busy shipping community, and armed vessels to ensure safe conduct. But trade did not improve. Although Elizabeth was as zealous for supremacy at sea as was her father, and although she encouraged the West-Country privateers, local traders were still much harassed.

The final clause of the charter had declared that it would become void if the Portreeve and the twelve burgesses failed to keep in good repair the harbour and the quay. But this was a mammoth task, for beach pebbles had by now almost filled the old harbour. Just a few years later, on 10 August 1562, the Council with much reluctance leased out the harbour, with its income, to John Dowding and his wife Joanna for a period of twenty-one years, for the sum of £8, to be paid quarterly.

One of the burgesses who signed this document was William Donnell. Less than three years later, on 4 February 1565 he, with the other burgesses, signed a letter from Robert Quirke, the customs controller for Minehead, to the Lord of the Manor, Thomas Luttrell, inviting him to become principal burgess of Minehead, in the hope that the Lord of the Manor would help them to repair the harbour. The Council feared that otherwise they would lose their Charter. A few weeks before this, Queen Elizabeth had ordered the ports around Bridgwater to be examined. Minehead had by now lost its former prosperity; only small trading vessels could now use the harbour, and customs dues had suffered, resulting in a loss to the Crown. The harbour was still blocked by a bank of stones washed up by the sea, even though the inhabitants were bound by the Charter to clear it annually.

The state of the harbour went from bad to worse. Some trade continued, notably with Wales and Ireland. But now most vessels had to discharge their cargo on the beach. This did not encourage the trade desperately needed to keep the port going. In 1570, however, Thomas Luttrell at last made a move, perhaps because he no longer had the use of a convenient harbour close to his seat at Dunster Castle. The landing place at Dunster Hawn had silted up and was no longer suitable for berthing the larger vessels now using the Channel, besides which there was very little shelter there. So he started a fund to build a new quay at Minehead, asking for contributions from his tenants, friends and neighbours. However, Thomas Luttrell died the following January, leaving an heir, George, who was only twelve years old.

By the close of Elizabeth's reign in 1603, £200 had been collected towards the new harbour, but little work had been done. This was mainly because seamen and ships had been commandeered for the Queen's service to defend the realm against the Spanish. In 1570 only two ships were reported to be in Minehead harbour: the *Margett* of 35 tons burden, and the *Saviour*, forty-six tons. No other ships were listed as being away, and of seamen, only five were on shore at the time the list was made. John Quirke was one of them. The others were away serving in the navy or trading in small boats.

In January 1602 a new enquiry began into the state of Minehead's port. This was instigated by the Exchequer, but prompted by a letter from George Luttrell, who had written to the Queen's Council informing them of his intention to build a new and better harbour, and stating that he would like to see the Charter of Minehead revoked. In addition to the £200 mentioned above collected by subscription, he was prepared to spend another £1,000 of his own money on building a totally new harbour. It was at this time that he had asked William Donnell to draw up the list of ships that used to use Minehead harbour before the town gained its Charter (as mentioned earlier in this chapter). He needed the list as proof of the deterioration of the fortunes of Minehead shipping while the town was a borough.

A rough draft of George Luttrell's letter to the Queen's Council is preserved among the Dunster Castle muniments. It reads in part as follows:
'Item 7. That before the grantings of the sayd Corporacion there was a very anciente and goode harbour there having 30 or 40 barques and boates belongeinge to the same ... [Marginal note inserted here] Whereas there are now but five, and that very meane.'

'... and great trafficke of merchandise used within the sayd towne and much mony payd to her majesty for the custom thereof, all now which is utterly decayed and impaired since the towne was incorporated to the great predidice of her Majesty and the hurt of the county and the loss of many lives and their goods'.

In Item 8, George Luttrell pointed out that 'the whole Manor and towne of Minhed, with the liberties and franchise thereof is the inheritance of George Luttrell, Esq., one of her Majesties Justices of the Peace within the Country of Somerset, who dwelleth very neere the sayd towne'. He added that he had in the last two years begun, at his own expense, to erect and make a new Harbour 'in a far better place than the former' and about 400 paces away from the existing one. In return he requested that Minehead's charter should be revoked. Once the new harbour was built, customs duties would increase, to the great benefit of the Crown, and Her Majesty's ships would be able to use the new port as a base for transporting soldiers, ammunition and supplies to Ireland.

It is not surprising that the Luttrell family wished to regain possession of the harbour at Minehead. The dues paid to them 'time out of mind' of one penny on every pound of wool, plus a further half-penny per stone weight for the use of the weighing beam in the town hall, had in the past brought in a goodly sum. They had also received smaller dues from loads of herrings, white fish, French or Spanish wine, whale oil, butter and other goods.

Although the Enquiry found that the burgesses had neglected their duty of keeping the harbour free of stones, so that it could hardly be used any more, Queen Elizabeth did not act on its findings. However, some years after his accession in 1603, James I did revoke the town's charter. In 1607 the rights of the manor of Minehead and its harbour were restored to the Luttrell family.

Some progress had already been made on the new harbour, marred by an accident in July 1605 when one David Cottle 'drowned in the New Key as he attempted to swim of Myne'. With the Luttrells in charge again, the rebuilding of the new harbour went ahead vigorously. In October 1609, George Luttrell wrote to William Morgan, asking him to invite forty named Minehead citizens to welcome his new ship to his new harbour, to give 'their benevolence to the furthering and ending of the new quay here'. But only twenty-three of those invited accepted, perhaps owing to resentment at the loss of Minehead's charter, and soon after, a few ungrateful merchants and ship-owners again petitioned the king, unsuccessfully, for its restoration.

It was recorded in the *Journal of the House of Commons* for 28 March 1610, in a bill passing through parliament for 'repairing and maintaining the quay or harbour of Minehead', that it had been built, at a cost of £5,000. But according to a plaque formerly on the quay, the work was not entirely finished until 1616, ten years after the death of William Donnell, then aged well over 100 years. The new harbour had cost George Luttrell far more than he expected, but it would bring about a new era of prosperity for Minehead.

Chapter Three: The Turbulent Seventeenth Century; Captain Nathaniel Bullocke and the *Patience* of Minehead

The focus of maritime activity now switched to the new harbour. Coal cellars and storehouses were built there, but only one survives. Built by Robert Quirke (Robert the Younger), this is now St Peter's-on-the-Quay. It is the remaining one of a pair; their rents paid for the upkeep of the almshouses Quirke built in Market Street in 1630. The story goes that in building the almshouses, Quirke was fulfilling a promise made to God when he was in danger of shipwreck during a violent storm.

Storms were just one of the problems facing the seventeenth-century mariners and merchants of Quay Town. This would be a turbulent century, with wars at home and abroad, and with the ever-present threat of piracy. Even so, the new harbour brought greater prosperity to Minehead. Trade increased and the town thrived. Merchants and master mariners built new houses, including some twelve in Quay Street. (Those houses which present a gable end to the street, such as the Old Harbour House, mostly date back to this time). Dwellings were even built beside the now redundant weir pool. A survey dated c.1740 notes buildings of various kinds with leases of 99 years from the Lord of the Manor dating back to the 17th century on both sides of Quay Street. The palatial 'Greate House' rented by Isett Quirke for £20 per annum, and formerly owned by Francis Webber, stood opposite the harbour but has not survived, nor have the buildings being built on the sea-side of the street or beyond the new harbour. Several red-herring houses (smokehouses) are mentioned: the shoals of herring now appearing in the Bristol Channel were another source of prosperity.

John Alloway, one of the Quaker merchant families, owned 'a very good dwelling house' in Quay Street. The *Red Lion*, with its cellars and red-herring houses, was one of several new inns which sprang up to serve thirsty seamen, such as the *Three Crowns*, the *Angel* and the *New Inn*, built into the side of the hill opposite what is now *The Old Ship Aground*.

Much of Minehead's prosperity was due to importing wool for the local cloth trade. Producing serge, broadcloth and other woven cloth was a thriving cottage industry in the West Country, and Minehead had been a 'staple port' since 1621, one of the few English ports licensed to import Irish wool. Welsh wool was also imported in large quantities. In October 1616, for instance, the *Harte* of Aberthaw sailed to Minehead with 30 stones of Welsh wool for a merchant in Milverton.

Little coal was imported at this date, as it came only from the estates of Welsh landed gentry. It was used partly for lime-burning or other agricultural uses. But large quantities of butter came over from the Vale of Glamorgan to Minehead and Barnstaple. The 187 kilderkins imported in 1616 (20,944 pounds weight) increased to 407 kilderkins (45,584 pounds) in 1635.

Other goods imported at this time through the new harbour included live sheep, pigs, cattle and horses. (The trade in live cattle from Ireland was later forbidden by Charles II. When in spite of this a shipment of live cattle arrived in Minehead in c.1669, they were sold and the money invested for the poor. This became known as the 'Cow Charity'.) It was more profitable to import these animals alive, so that the buyers could use their hides, offal and other by-products as well as the meat. The hides, tanned or raw, were exported in their turn, along with a variety of other animal skins such as deer, calf and rabbit, and even dog skins. Much of the trade was up and down the Bristol Channel: the danger from storms and shipwreck was often preferable to transporting goods overland, as the roads were so bad that at times they were impassable.

Trade with the rest of the world was also increasing: goods from France, Spain and even the West Indies found their way to Minehead harbour. This increased the variety of exports to South Wales, which in 1620 included broadcloth, serge and kersey cloth; brandy, cider, Spanish wine, pipes and tobacco; powders and perfume and 'apothecary wares', besides locally-made reap-hooks, shovels and cart wheels; groceries, earthenware, candles and soap. Since Minehead's charter had been revoked, the Luttrells again received harbour dues from all these items, though these were now often double what they had been, due to inflation. For every bullock to or from Wales, the Lords of the Manor received one penny, while every pig cost one half-penny and every horse, two pennies. These dues were intended to go towards keeping the harbour in good repair.

Merchants and seamen such as Robert Quirke and Alexander Leakey were typical of those now made prosperous by trading from Minehead. Besides building the almshouses, Robert Quirke the Younger gave to St Michael's Church the painted boards depicting the Ten Commandments, the Creed and the Lord's Prayer that still hang there today. The fortunes of Alexander Leakey, who lived in a large house on Quay Street, probably mirror those of many Minehead merchants at this time. Customs records for the later 1620s and early 1630s show that business was booming. On ships such as the *Charity*, the *Godspeed*, the *Blessing*, the *Emmanuel*, the *Jane* and the *Elizabeth* (his wife's name), Leakey transported timber and tar from Bristol to ports further down the coast, and brought salt, wine and vinegar from Brittany in return for tallow and coal. His main trade, though, was in wool, which he imported from southern Ireland, especially from Youghal, near Cork, which seems to have been the main port used by Minehead merchants in this trade. To Ireland he took cereals and beans, with some light-weight luxury goods such as mercery and haberdashery for the aristocracy.

Alexander Leakey's prosperity did not last. He lost many ships in the treacherous Irish Sea, and did no trade at all in 1635-6. From being the sixth wealthiest man in Minehead in 1624, and a leading citizen, he fell to 120th in 1642 and died the following year. Local legend ascribes the loss of his ships to tempests summoned by his mother. The ghost of 'Old Mother Leakey' was said to have whistled up fierce adverse winds, causing his ships to capsize. But storms were frequent in those seas, and there were other factors threatening Minehead's prosperity during this difficult century, such as the ill-advised English campaigns against Spain in 1625 and France in 1627, and this was just the beginning. The nations of England, France, Holland and Spain were constantly at war with each other throughout the century.

Another huge threat to merchant shipping was piracy. Barbary pirates from the Algerian coast, commonly known as 'Turks', had been a menace to shipping on the high seas since the early sixteenth century, when the Moors were expelled from Spain. These pirate ships often included in their crews Christian European sailors, including some from Britain. After King James I came to the throne, British privateers were no longer encouraged to attack Spanish ships. Many were reluctant to give up this lucrative profession and joined 'Turkish' ships.

West Country vessels trading with Ireland were especially vulnerable, and even in the Bristol Channel itself, ships were captured, their goods seized and their crews and passengers taken to Algeria to be sold as slaves. In West Country parish registers there are many examples of financial aid being given to people who had been captured and enslaved by the 'Turks' but who managed to get home again, safe but penniless. Spanish, Dutch and French privateers were also eager to seize ships, their cargoes and their crews.

King Charles's navy was unable to cope. So in 1627 two Minehead men, Captains Thomas Lee and Hugh Davis, obtained letters of marque from the king for their ships, the 60-ton *Elizabeth* and the 30-ton *James,* to protect Minehead's important trade with Ireland. The king was also petitioned for permission to arm a ship to protect vessels using the Bristol Channel from the Turkish men-of-war. A ship bearing the somewhat inappropriate name of *Dove,* was soon fitted out and seems to have been successful in clearing the Channel of this threat. However, having accomplished her mission, the *Dove* set out on a privateering expedition of her own. She took a Portuguese ship as a prize, but was herself captured by a Dutch privateer and sunk. Her sailors were briefly imprisoned in Madeira, used as a captive crew by the Dutch captain, and finally reached home via Rotterdam. Other Minehead ships were more successful in bringing their prizes home; so much so, that a King's Receiver, Sir John Drake, was appointed to claim five per cent of their treasure for the Crown.

Minehead was one of twenty-four western seaports told to fortify itself against a possible Spanish invasion in 1626; in 1634-5, the town had to contribute £60 to arm a ship of 800 tons, carrying 260 soldiers for King Charles's navy. Once the war with France had begun, seamen in Minehead faced a new threat which continued for most of the century: the press gangs, authorized to seize sailors by force to man the state's warships.

During the Civil War, which began with the Irish rebellion in 1641, the sympathies of most Minehead citizens were with the Parliamentarians, as were those of Thomas Luttrell II and his wife Jane, who refused to surrender Dunster Castle to the Royalists. When the Marquis of Hertford, sent to recruit Somerset men for the Royalist army, marched to Minehead with 160 or so soldiers, intending to commandeer vessels to take himself and his men to Wales, his intentions were foiled by the Lord of the Manor. Thomas is said to have ordered all the vessels in the harbour to remove their rudders. The Marquis was forced to take refuge from the hostile townspeople in 'a strong inn' along with his followers and their horses. On hearing of the approach of the Parliament's Lord Lieutenant of Somerset, he and his recruits managed to escape in two Welsh coal boats, while the mounted officers made their way to Cornwall over Exmoor.

The tables were turned in January 1643 when Royalist ships commandeered in Wales blockaded Minehead harbour, holding back supplies of coal and provisions. Thomas Luttrell frightened off a raiding party that reached Dunster Castle after having already caused trouble in Minehead. However by 1646 the Royalist cause seemed to be winning, prompting the now sick Lord of the Manor to surrender his castle to the King. It remained in Royalist hands until April that year. When it surrendered after a long siege, Minehead bells rang to celebrate the end of the war in Somerset, and soon after, the collapse of the Royalist army in England.

The end of the English Civil War in 1646 did not mean peace for the country and its trading ships. The defeat of King Charles I and his execution in 1649 made many European countries our enemies. French ships, both state-owned and privateers, patrolled the Bristol Channel in search of defenceless merchant ships, seizing thousands of tons of British shipping, and taking off over half-a-million pounds-worth of merchandise. Catholic Ireland had rebelled against the Parliamentarians, and, it was feared, could become a base from which the Royalists could launch an attack on England.

Even during the Civil War, Minehead had been sending men, horses and supplies to the garrisons in Ireland, which had greatly added to the town's prosperity. Francis Bishop's ship the *John*, for instance, was paid £14.13s. to deliver shoes, stockings, caps and coats for the soldiers serving there. Merchant families that did well from trading with southern Ireland were now establishing themselves in Minehead. These included Samuel Crockford's family which settled in Quay Street, and the Hayman family, who had a second house at the Quay, the lease of which was rated in 1655 at the high figure of £40.

Cromwell began to assemble a huge army and Minehead harbour became a major port of embarcation for Ireland. However, the need to quarter the soldiers while a huge army was assembled, along with the difficulties caused to shipping by the French ships, plunged the inhabitants of towns along the North Devon and Somerset coasts into severe poverty. The Irish trade was badly affected, and the trade with South Wales fell away too as vessels were commandeered by the government. Hundreds of Irish refugees fled to ports such as Minehead. Going by the population figures alone, the town and port would have seemed to be thriving. However, these figures were swollen by the Irish refugees and the numbers of soldiers billeted throughout the town.

Not all ships seized to carry Cromwell's army arrived in Ireland safely. The records of the Somerset Quarter Sessions for 1649 include the following sad story:

'The humble petition of the inhabitants of the towne and parish of Minehead ... Humbly sheweth, That six ships and barques of the towne being imprest in the year 1649 for the transportation of soldiers and horses for the service of Minehead, did on the 5th january of that sayd year satt sayle from this harbour and within two days after in a greeat tempest five of the sayd ships and barques were cast away on the coste of Ireland, by means whereof there were neere 100 poore widowwes and father less children ... trading hath of layt fayled both by sea and land ... Beside all these things, this poore town has been much burdened by many poore distressed peopl which were enforced out of ireland by means of the late rebellion there. And several shippinge belonging to the towne have of late years bin taken by men-of-warre to the great damage of the owners.'

The dangers to shipping included the 'Turks' and Spanish privateers in the Bristol Channel. Petitions were sent to the Admiralty Commissioners from local seaports, begging for a man-of-war and nimble frigates to be sent to defend the Bristol Channel coast from this threat. But nothing was done, for the war in Ireland was considered a more urgent priority. Captain Swanley, Admiral of the Irish Seas, ordered that all vessels that were available and sea-worthy were to be 'imprest' in the service of the government for transporting soldiers and horses to Ireland. One man chosen to carry out these orders in Minehead was Nathaniel Bullocke, captain and master of the barque *Patience.*

Nathaniel Bullocke must have been a familiar figure in Quay Town, for on his appointment as a local Press Officer in 1649, it was stated that he had over thirty years' experience in sail from Minehead trading with ports such as Youghal, Cork and Kinsale in Ireland. In February 1647, for instance, he was recorded as having brought a cargo of wool to Minehead Quay from Youghal. Probably born in around 1610, he was not a Minehead man, going by the church records, for he was the first of his name to live in the town. Most probably he hailed from Barnstaple or Bideford way, serving as a boy in the Bar Fleet, a large fleet of bluff-bowed, square-rigged craft working along the western coasts. Such hardy craft were as accustomed to beaching on remote shingle banks as to coming alongside rough stone jetties. Minehead probably drew Nathaniel because of its new harbour and its berthing facilities, which were superior to the other ports on the North Devon and Somerset coast.

Being a Press Officer, forcing private vessels and unwilling sailors into government service, did not make Nathaniel Bullocke very popular in Minehead. On one occasion he fell out with no less a personage than Robert Quirke, son of Robert Quirke the Younger. Bullocke's *Patience,* on its return to Minehead after sailing down the coast to Ilfracombe to 'impress' ships and sailors, needed repairs and Bullocke asked some carpenters working on one of Quirke's ships to come and repair his own. When Quirke discovered this, he was furious, and set about the Press Officer with a cudgel. We know this from a petition Nathaniel Bullocke sent to the Justices of the Peace at Ilchester.

On the other hand, several people were kind enough to warn him not to bring the *Patience* into harbour one day in 1653, because the 'Press' was on the Quay. The two Press Officers concerned complained to the Admiralty Commissioners that Nathaniel Bullocke had stayed out of the harbour, although 'he was already in the service, but refused to show his pass'. Whether he was becoming wary of government service or returning from a trading expedition of his own, no document that has survived can tell us. In December of the same year he married Jane Webber and settled down in Quay Town.

Minehead trading fleets, along with those from ports as far down the coast as Bideford, were now suffering so badly from attacks by pirates and enemy warships (for Cromwell was at war with the Dutch and the Spanish) that the Navy Commissioners, in response to a petition sent by Robert Quirke and fourteen others, finally provided escort vessels: the *Lion,* which escorted ships trading with Ireland, and the *Harp* with its eight to ten guns. Their efforts were later aided by other frigates such as the *Fox* and the *Dartmouth.* Cromwell also eventually dealt successfully with the pirate menace by sending a well-equipped expedition to the Algerian coast, which destroyed Barbary ports and freed the British slaves. All this activity finally succeeded in keeping the seas clear, and trade began to pick up.

The Restoration of the Monarchy in 1660 ended the wars in Europe and secured peace in Ireland. Trade with Ireland could and did flourish, and the Irish nobility as well as cargoes travelled safely back and forth in Minehead ships. Between 1660 and 1667, a fishing fleet set out from Minehead each year for Newfoundland. But England was still at war with the Dutch, and warships were needed to protect the convoys of up to thirty ships sailing up and down the Bristol Channel, some from as far away as Virginia, on their way to Bristol. A new treaty with Algeria generally kept the 'Turks', who had recommenced their activities with the Restoration, away from the Bristol Channel, but they still attacked ships bound for Newfoundland. Increased action by the British navy at the end of the century did away almost completely with this threat, but even in the early eighteenth century, a few attacks occurred.

It was not only improved and safer trade that was enriching the merchants of Quay Town. Duties on imported goods reached such a high level in the second half of the century that smuggling became a tempting source of income for even apparently respectable families. Even Colonel Frances Luttrell, who had succeeded to the Lordship of the Manor, seems to have been implicated, judging by his unwillingness to investigate supposed offences and his readiness to punish informers such as one Peter Bond, who told the authorities in 1682 that wine and brandy had been hidden in Samual Crockford's home cellar in Quay Street. Likewise bales of cloth had been hauled into the courtyard of Thomas Wilson's home, also near the Quay, and Captain Isaac Davis had concealed contraband in his ship the *Diligence*. Some customs officers were inclined to turn a blind eye and share the profits, while informers were treated as if they were the ones breaking the law. Peter Bond, for instance, was imprisoned for three nights and then publicly whipped in the market place, no doubt as an example to others.

Captain Nathaniel Bullocke was not implicated in any of these illegal activities, as far as we know. In 1667 he had become the father of a second daughter, Hanna. His first daughter, Elizabeth, was by now twelve years old. Jane died in childbirth two years later: her baby Hanna was baptised the same day as the entry was made in the Burial Register. Bullocke traded on; there are numerous records of voyages to and from Minehead in the *Patience*. He must have married again by 1672, though there is no evidence of this in Minehead registers, for his first son, William, was born in May that year. William died during the winter of 1674 and is buried in Minehead churchyard. A further daughter, named Jane after his first wife, was born in December 1681.

There is no further record of his second wife; all subsequent entries in the Registers refer to the growing family of Nathaniel and Elizabeth Bullocke. The Captain seems to have retired by 1682, when another son,

Nathaniel, was born, as there is no further mention of the *Patience* in Minehead harbour records. Two more daughters followed in 1864 and 1687, while in 1689, a further son, John, was born.

Meanwhile a new king of England, James II, had been crowned in February 1685. As he was an avowed Roman Catholic, it was feared that he might try to re-impose his faith on the country. The Protestant Duke of Monmouth, Charles II's illegitimate son, landed in Dorset a few months later, hoping to gain enough support to depose the Catholic monarch and reign in his stead. He was well received in the West Country and proclaimed king at Taunton. Finding himself under attack at Bridgwater, he apparently sent two troops of horse to Minehead to collect six guns from the harbour with which to defend himself. These guns must have been in position for some time, to defend the harbour against pirates. But Monmouth was defeated at the Battle of Sedgemoor before the guns could reached him. They seem to have been abandoned by their escort somewhere along the road.

James II fled into exile a few years later, when William of Orange was invited to reign over the country. The first war against Louis XIV followed soon after. Although peace was made with France in 1697, the War of the Spanish Succession would soon again arouse fears of invasion. It would be another sixteen years before Minehead ships would be able to trade in peace.

Captain Bullocke died aged almost ninety years old in 1696 and was buried on 15th August. Elizabeth followed him in 1704. He had lived through a turbulent century, in a town and a calling that were much affected by the troubles of his day. More than once he had faced total ruin. He lost his first wife at a time when he most needed her, and when his future seemed far from secure. He worked in Minehead when the town was at one of its lowest points and yet lived to see it become a stable and important Bristol Channel port. Deeply carved into the south door of St Michael's Church, along with other marks, are the initials NB. Unlikely, of course, but could this be a tangible reminder of this tough old seaman?

Chapter Four: Prosperity to Decline: the Eighteenth Century

At the beginning of the eighteenth century, Minehead was a thriving port, with thirty ships of over fifteen tons registered here. The harbour could comfortably accommodate ships of 300 and 400 tons. Large quantities of wool were imported from Ireland: over forty ships were engaged in this trade. Coal from South Wales was another major import. Other ships sailed as far as Virginia and the West Indies. Minehead also gave shelter from storms to ships passing up and down the Bristol Channel. These had to pay one or two shillings per tide for this refuge, if British; other ships would pay more. For larger ships on their way to or from Bristol from Asia or Africa, the charge was ten shillings. With its improved harbour, Minehead was reckoned 'a safe port in a storm', and local seamen boasted that even during the great storm of 1703, which damaged ships in all the other harbours of West Somerset, those sheltering in the harbour here suffered little or no damage.

Huge herring shoals were another source of wealth for Minehead and its fishermen. Shoals had begun to appear in great numbers in the estuary during the previous century, and by the beginning of this century, 4,000 barrels of herring, especially smoked herring, were being exported annually to Portugal, Spain, Italy and beyond. There were many small smokehouses along Quay Street, and at least two of them remain, behind numbers 11a and 43. Others were on the sea side of the street. According to Savage's *History of the Hundred of Carhampton,* there were three 'red-herring houses' by the King's Arms public house, and another behind the Quay itself. Minehead was famous for its herrings: 'herrings and bread ring the bells of Minehead', ran the words of an old song.

Trade was so brisk that the sailing ships often had to berth three or four abreast. It must have been a wonderful sight. The port gave employment to not just seamen but loaders and unloaders; customs officials; merchants and their clerks; ropemakers (there is still a road called Hemp Garden in Higher Town) and chandlers. Naturally there were several alehouses and inns, especially as at that time wages were paid partly in beer. Loading and unloading was thirsty work and of course there was no proper supply of drinking water. In about 1737, public houses by the harbour included the Lamb, the King's Arms and the New Inn, while the Red Lion and the Star were further along Quay Street. Some of these were new, others had changed their names, as frequently occurred.

Foreign enemies still threatened this prosperous port, however. The wars against the French, halted briefly by a treaty in 1697, resumed in 1702. They would continue for over ten years. Concerned by the lack of defences for the harbour, for the six guns requisitioned by the Duke of Monmouth had not been returned, Minehead's MPs, Jacob Bancks and

Alexander Luttrell, appealed to William III for help. They pointed out that during the truce, Irish and French privateers visiting the town had noted its lack of defences and had boasted of returning to sack it if war resumed. Ten guns were requested: there were already bases for seven and an extension planned to the harbour wall would have room for three more. The town would provide gunners and powder.

Seventy-five inhabitants of Minehead signed this petition, and it was supported by the principal Customs Officer, Thomas Wolstenholme, who shrewdly pointed out the danger faced by the Customs House, where 'all the King's books, bonds and papers' could be destroyed by fire if the quay was not defended. The response was positive, helped perhaps by the fact that Jacob Banks was a retired captain of the British navy, and Thomas Wolstenholme's brother was a friend of the Lord Treasurer. Douglas J. Stevens' booklet about the harbour guns lists the huge amount of equipment sent, besides the ten big guns and their carriages. The war would end in 1713, before the extension to the harbour was ready; the three superfluous guns were taken away for use elsewhere.

During these wars at least three ships from Minehead gained letters of marque: the 200-ton *Queen Anne* (Anne became queen in 1702), owned by Andrew and David Hare and William Alloway; Captain William Hayman's 100-ton *Wincanton*, and the 100-ton *Three Brothers*, captained by William Rogers and owned by his brothers Edward and James. She carried thirty men and eight guns, as well as all kinds of small arms and enough food for nine months. Privateering could be very profitable as although captured French ships had to be sold and the money given to the Crown, the crew were usually generously rewarded.

George Luttrell's 'new' quay was at risk from natural as well as human forces. The sea itself was a danger to the harbour, not only through violent storms, but also from longshore drift from the west. There was increasingly less depth in the harbour even at high tide, and the pebble bank at the end of the harbour wall was growing in size. The pebbles were carted away at low tide and dumped in the sea. But the next vigorous south-westerly would dump more pebbles and the bank would rise again. (Even nowadays this pebble bank is a problem; it has to be cleared regularly.)

In 1682 Colonel Frances Luttrell, at his own expense, had had huge rocks brought by sea to the western side of the harbour, to reinforce it. This date was marked by a plaque which has now disappeared, though the rocks are still visible at low tide. But before the end of the seventeenth century, Minehead harbour was again silting up and threatened to become unusable by the bigger ships. Colonel Luttrell died in 1690, to be succeeded by Tregonwell Luttrell, then aged only six. His mother Mary had taken Jacob (later Sir Jacob) Bancks as her second husband, and in 1701 he commissioned a survey of the harbour. This found that during neap tides the harbour was only twenty-two feet deep.

The surveyor, Thomas Surbey, drew up a rough map of the harbour and its setting (now in the Somerset Heritage Centre). He proposed extending the curve of the harbour wall to give protection from the east-north-east winds as well as from the prevailing westerlies. New 'backwork' would be added to strengthen this extension, and groynes would be put in on the beach behind the harbour and close to it, to slow down the longshore drift of pebbles. Two 'stops or cheques' were to jut out from the sea wall on the landward entrance to the harbour to prevent easterly winds from making a whirlpool, which, he had been informed 'often forces ships to sink one another'! To the east of the harbour, he suggested also putting a 'stop or cheque' in the form of two joined poles, as he had been informed by some seamen that a dangerous swell sometimes came from the south-east. However, others had said this was not a problem, and Surbey wisely added 'if the latter be true then this need not be erected'. It was not true, and the 'cheques' were not needed. Otherwise the plan to extend the harbour was eventually carried out, though it would see many delays. The place where the old and new wall join can easily be seen in the stonework on the inner side of the wall.

Thomas Surbey's plan shows that the old jetty had all but disappeared and was now just a heap of beach stones, though some of the old sluice pool remained. Houses had been built around it, as well as along Quay Street on both sides towards the harbour. At this end, according to the plan, the houses appear more spaced out and depicted as larger than the ones at the town end: these were likely to have been the houses of merchants or master mariners. It is interesting to see from the plan that there was once a bowling green on Culvercliffe, and what may be a pond, and in fact there was a pond on this site in living memory.

When Tregonwell died in 1703, his uncle Alexander Luttrell became Lord of the Manor, and it was he who arranged for the new head to be built onto the end of the harbour wall. An Act of Parliament had already been passed in 1701 to allow the Lord of the Manor to increase duties on certain items in order to pay for these improvements for the next twenty-one years, as in spite of Minehead's success as a trading port in the last century, income from duties did not keep up with the cost to the Luttrells of keeping the harbour in good condition.

In 1704 Alexander Luttrell contracted one Daniel Dennell from Cannington to build a new head 120 feet long, to be made of a wooden framework filled with stones. A 100-foot groyne was also to be built, to keep back the drifting pebbles. The work was supposed to take eighteen months, but took six or seven years, by which time the timber framework had been eaten into by woodworm. Meanwhile, in 1711 Alexander Luttrell had died and his son, also named Alexander, was still a minor. His widow, Dorothy, took on the project, although the costs were rising yearly and were well below any income from the harbour dues. Supported by some local merchants, she obtained from parliament an extension of the right to levy increased duties to help pay for further improvements to the harbour. This was granted on condition that a large lantern be affixed to the quay head, and kept burning at night between 1st September and 31st March. Later this lantern was replaced by a pier-head light, regularly inspected by Trinity House officials at the time Hancock was writing his history of Minehead (1903).

A new contract to build a strong stone wall to encase the timber frame was signed with Dennell in 1713, but he proved unable to keep his promises. He kept demanding more money than had been agreed, and in the end, walked away from the project altogether without paying his workmen. A new supervisor, Joseph Alloway, a merchant from the prominent Minehead Quaker family, was appointed in 1714 and the work went ahead again, using the same mason, Thomas Chidgey of Watchet and his men. Alloway succeeded where Dennell had failed. By Christmas, his workers had completed the outer wall, and the following year they encased the inner wall of the harbour too. Partly at his own expense, Alloway used cranes to fix huge timbers to the inside wall and also built groynes to counter the longshore drift of pebbles.

The new harbour wall had to be repaired again the following Christmas, after a terrible storm destroyed the part facing the sea, as well as damaging the wharf and several houses in Quay Street. Thomas Chidgey was now instructed to build a long higher wall, the New Head, that summer, and to raise the old quay wall by six feet. The cost to Dorothy Luttrell had been great but Minehead harbour now prospered. The pebbles still had to be carted away regularly, at some expense, but even the larger ships could again use the harbour. Trade was even greater than when the new harbour was first built. Ten officers were based at the Customs House, and Lady Luttrell easily fought off Watchet's request to become, like Minehead, a staple port allowed to import wool from Ireland.

The town, too, especially its merchants, prospered because of the new harbour; the population had increased to the point where some Minehead men felt that the town should regain its charter and govern itself. Successive petitions to Queen Anne and her successor George I have survived, but none were granted. It was very clear that only the Luttrells had the resources to look after the harbour which was largely the cause of the town's prosperity.

In his *History of Minehead*, Hancock quotes the novelist Daniel Defoe, who visited Minehead in 1722 as part of a tour of Britain and was impressed by the new harbour. 'Minehead is the best port and the safest harbour on this side of all these counties. No ship is so big, but that it may come in; and no weather so bad, but the ships are safe when they are in', he wrote. Although trade was chiefly with Ireland, there was some too with Virginia and the West Indies, and other foreign trade through

Bristol and Barnstaple. Defoe considered the town was well-built and full of rich merchants. He attributed its prosperity mainly to the Acts of Parliament, by now renewed several times, which had given the Luttrells powers to maintain and improve the harbour.

Wool continued to be a mainstay of trade until the second half of the century. Between 1718 and 1740 an average of about 10,000 stone was imported from Ireland. Linen, hides and skins were also imported, along with coal and culm from South Wales. Of the exports, oak bark and grain were reckoned the most important. There was still trade to the West Indies and Virginia, some via Bristol and Barnstaple. Minehead harbour also gained income from giving shelter from storms to larger ships making for Bristol, as no other harbour on this coast was deep enough.

In spite of such prosperity, smuggling in brandy, tobacco and, strangely enough, Irish soap, still tempted many people. A blind eye was turned by the customs officials, many of whom were local men appointed by the very Minehead traders who sold the smuggled goods. So great was the problem that Minehead was described as 'the fountain which supplies the whole country with Irish soap and other run'd [sic] goods'. Any zealous customs officer was removed by some means or other, with the gentry not interfering, either because they were benefitting or for fear of losing votes.

The cost of maintaining the harbour continued to grow, and it proved impossible to finally pay off the debts incurred by the Luttrells for the building of the 'New Head' in Queen Anne's reign. The trustees appointed by the Luttrells to collect dues and use them to maintain the port had to obtain a new loan in 1770 from the then Lord of the Manor, Henry Fownes Luttrell. By the end of the century, the debt had grown to £20,000, in spite of keelage charges having been increased.

Storms continued to cause damage to the harbour wall, especially in spring 1741, when several houses at the quay were destroyed, the road was made impassable, and the quay wall needed major repairs. In 1770, £200-worth of damage was done. The job of regularly clearing away the stones from the harbour was also very expensive, and sometimes cost more than the income from the port: the over-run between 1753 and 1756 was close to £100. In 1755 the job needed eighteen men and two carters with their horses, along with four 'tossers'. These presumable had the hardest job, that of emptying the baskets of stones into the carts, for they were paid one shilling and a penny a day, compared to the labourers' pay of ten pence. In 1773, the ale supplied for the labourers cost as much as their pay.

Meanwhile the harbour continued to silt up. At the end of 1753 the maximum depth was registered as 27 feet 6 inches. However, the harbour was still able to comfortably accommodate large vessels. The fifteen or so ships recorded there on one day included two foreign merchant ships and one of the largest vessels belonging to Minehead, Captain Gregory's *Molly*. There were other problems too. The high keelage charges necessary to help pay for the upkeep of the harbour may have begun to deter ships from using Minehead; charges at Porlock and Watchet were lower.

The next chapter follows the fortunes of some of the trading smacks that used Minehead well into the nineteenth century. However, trade was declining, and by the end of the century, the high days of Minehead as a port were over. By 1790, vessels no longer went to the West Indies; even the Irish trade had diminished, as the woollen trade with Ireland had faded away. The Irish refugees who had fled to Minehead and the West Country during the Irish Wars wisely learnt to weave and spin during their exile. On their return they now processed themselves the wool they used to export to England. Bay yarn and animal hides and skins continued to be imported, in lessening amounts, along with butter and linen, but only three ships, the *Whitworth*, the *Britannia* and the *Effort*, still sailed to Cork and Waterford. The trade was now mainly across to Wales or up and down the Channel: nine 'coasters' were listed as belonging to Minehead in 1790, including the *Industry*, whose fortunes are told in the next chapter.

Boat-building continued for a while, on the beach or at Manston's yard, just beyond the harbour wall. But from about mid-century, the number and size of vessels using the harbour began to decline. A visitor in 1800 noted that Minehead's quayside and harbour, once busy with ships trading abroad and along the coast, was now but a shadow of its former self. The population of Quay Town diminished and some houses fell into ruin. John Collinson, in his book on the history and antiquities of Somerset, published in 1791, claimed that whereas in 1705 there were 64 occupied houses with 452 inhabitants in Quay Town, by 1783 only 45 houses were occupied, housing 226 people.

The decline of Minehead as a port had a dire effect on the whole town. The population declined; poverty was widespread. Poor harvests, and the impossibility of importing food during the wars with Napoleon, made things worse. The Great Fire of 1791 was not the only fire in Minehead around this time. A visitor to the harbour in 1813 noted the unrepaired blackened walls of burnt cottages and a total lack of activity at the previously busy harbour.

The Industrial Revolution, which was beginning to gather momentum in the second half of the century, was a major factor in Minehead's decline as a port. The new larger vessels and later, steamships, no longer called at Minehead, where there were neither space nor facilities for them; they carried on up the Channel to Bristol. Ilfracombe was overtaking Minehead as a port, too. By 1830 trade had become much more local: grain, malt, bark, timber, flour and some leather were shipped to Bristol, bringing back mainly groceries on the return trip. Other ships crossed the Channel to Wales with flour, malt and timber, bringing back coal, limestone and culm to fire the limestone kilns. The lime was spread on local fields or transported inland.

By 1834 Minehead had ceased to be a Registry Port in its own right, with jurisdiction over Porlock and Watchet: all three now came under the Registry Port of Bridgwater.

To make matters worse, the herring shoals suddenly disappeared at the end of the eighteenth century, to reappear only rarely and spasmodically in the Bristol Channel. Just this year, for instance, in January 2012, a Quay-Town man went fishing and found his nets suddenly full of herrings. He remembered his grandfather also having occasionally landed huge numbers from time to time. Perhaps this is why some of the smaller, domestic smokehouses survived.

The decline in trade and the loss of the herring industry could have had disastrous consequences for the whole town. Fortunately, however, Minehead was about to experience a complete change of direction; it was beginning to forge a new identity for itself as a seaside resort.

Schooner Pemilon off white mark.   John Sulman

Chapter Five: Minehead Trading Sloops and Smacks

We hear a great deal about the voyages of the larger schooners and ketches, voyages to almost every port in the West of England, to Ireland, France, the Mediterranean and even across the Atlantic. Yet a very important contribution to the general pattern of coastwise trade was made by the trading sloop, or smack. Emerging in the eighteenth century, and crowding the little harbours along the North Devon and Somerset coasts during the nineteenth, these little fore-and-aft-rigged trading vessels carried a vast percentage of West Country trade.

Some of these vessels were technically known as sloops, but by 1825 or so, the term 'smack' was used as a generally inclusive term, and will be so used in this chapter. (See Chapter Nine for more about sloops and smacks.)

It was the smack that bore the weight of local trade within the bounds of the Bristol Channel and the smack that went shopping to Bristol for the smaller communities along the coast, enabling each port to establish itself as a centre for the exchange of light domestic industry.

It was the smack that plied to and fro from the ports and beaches of the Welsh coast to the smaller creeks and beaches of the Exmoor coast, inaccessible to larger craft. It was also the smack that established the fast passenger services to Bristol and the major ports of South Wales. In fact the smacks pursued their everyday tasks unnoticed in the background of port activity.

It was a great advantage that a smack could be built almost anywhere. If the farmer's land went down to the sea, then he might have a small smack beached below his fields as well as a waggon or two in his cart sheds. He needed limestone for his fields and coal to burn it and it was a lot cheaper to fetch it himself than to ask at the Quay. John Redd, for instance, of Broomstreet Farm not only built his own lime kilns but owned his own vessels and later ran a coal business too.

From the *Unanimity* of the late eighteenth century to the little *Harriet Ann* that later regularly brought thirty tons of coal across the Channel to the gasworks in Quay West, the smack reigned supreme for centuries.
One reason why today the smacks are almost forgotten while an interest is still maintained in the larger schooners and ketches may be because the size, lines and speed of the larger vessels have always captured the imagination of casual observers. And there is no doubt that the tops'l schooner *Trio* of Watchet or the *Flying Foam* of Bridgwater, reaching up the Channel under all sail with a following westerly breeze, must have made an impressive sight, while the smack *M & E* of Minehead pursuing her way heavily laden with coal formed a less romantic picture. This

chapter, however, will concentrate on the humble but indispensable smack.

The names of many vessels are preserved in the Port Books of Minehead in the Somerset Heritage Centre, Taunton. The earliest mention of a trading smack appears in a bundle of papers and receipts for June 1785. This vessel, the *Industry*, is fairly well documented until she was wrecked in September 1799, so she will give us a good idea of the kind of vessel trading out of Minehead in the eighteenth century.

The *Industry* was owned by John Fownes Luttrell, then Lord of the Manor, and was employed in carrying coal, culm (coal dust for firing lime kilns) and limestone from the Welsh ports of Tenby, Aberthaw and Barry to Minehead. It is not known how old the *Industry* was when she began trading for John Fownes Luttrell, but repairs undertaken by the local shipyard and the expenses incurred then indicate that she was by no means a new vessel. The following information, taken from the accounts of the shipwright, Thomas Manston of Minehead, and the vessel's master, Richard Richards, relate to the preparations made towards making the vessel ready for sea. In an extensive document relating to the repairs done in Manston's yard, just west of the harbour, for the years 1784 and 1785, the following entry is found for 22 January 1785: 'began the repairs to the sloop'.

That this is indeed the *Industry* is made clear by the bill presented to Mr Luttrell by Thomas Manston the day after the refitted *Industry* sailed for the coast of South Wales for a cargo of stone:

Account of the stuff used in repairs of the smack Industry. July 6th 1785

		£	s	d
For 17 feet of 2½ inch Oak plank at 5d	....	0	7	1
For 437 feet of 2 inch Oak plank at 4d.	...	7	5	8
For 368 feet of ½ inch Oak plank at 3d.	...	4	12	8
For 900 Trunnels at 3'6 per Hundred	...	1	11	6
For 3 Dozen of Wedges at 1'4 per doz	...	0	4	0
		14	0	11

Trunnels (tree nails) are wooden pegs used instead of iron nails in ships because they would not rust.

A week earlier Captain Richards had been to the sail loft of William Padley of Minehead in order to have some work done on the fores'l:

		£	s	d
To 10 ¼ yards canvas at 17 ½d. per foot	...	0	15	4
To adding a cloth in the foresail	...	0	4	2
		0	19	6

By the amount of timber used in the repairs it appears that the *Industry* underwent little short of a major refit. However, as she was hauling stone and coal, and beaching on shingle and boulders on almost every other trip, it is hardly surprising that the timbers of such vessels required constant attention. Many years later another stout Minehead smack, the *John & William*, built especially for the Bristol Channel trade at Porlock Weir in 1858, would capsize after unloading a cargo of limestone from the beach near Barry in 1894.

The newly-refitted *Industry* made four voyages in July 1785. The first was on 5 July to near Aberthaw; the second, on the 12th, to Tenby, and the third and fourth to Aberthaw on 20th and 28th July. With the exception of the voyage to Tenby for a cargo of coal, all the voyages were made for limestone.

Mr Luttrell owned extensive tracts of land with very little limestone, so it is reasonable to assume that one of the major reasons for refitting the *Industry* was to supply the local need for limestone, which was burned in kilns for use as an agricultural fertilizer. A busy trade became established across the Channel from the limestone cliffs of South Wales to the limestone-poor areas of North Devon and West Somerset. Early in the nineteenth century a dozen kilns were working along the coast from the Foreland to Dunster beach. You can still see some former Minehead kilns, with their wide arches, in Quay West.

Richard Richards had been engaged by Mr Luttrell early on as master of the *Industry*, at a salary of two pounds a month. As he could write a good hand, Captain Richards, besides being an able seaman, could deal with the paperwork required by Mr Luttrell. We are indebted to the careful way in which he recorded every transaction made in the early months of his command, such as his record for 6 July 1785 of the purchase of a lantern, at 2s.6d; a tin candlestick, for 1s.2d, and a tin pint, costing fourpence.

As she left Minehead harbour on her first voyage since her refit, on 5 July 1785, the *Industry* would have been pulled slowly out by the hobbling crew. Hobblers were small boats and their crews which towed larger vessels in and out of harbours during the era of sailing ships. As the *Industry*'s patched canvas tautened under a steady breeze, the towing hawser would have been slackened off and she was outward bound towards the coast of Wales, just visible on the horizon. That morning before sailing, Captain Richards had been visited by William Gale, Mr Luttrell's agent, and paid the four pounds owing to him for two months' wages.

It was to William Gale that Captain Richards would have presented his accounts on his return, once he had paid off the man and boy who had sailed with him. By the time Captain Richards returned from his next voyage, a receipt would have been made out for the correct amount, to be given to him by William Gale at the quayside.

One voyage for which we have both the voyage account and the receipts from the port of call is a voyage made to Tenby on 12 July 1785. These papers included the Bond Certificate relating to the duty imposed on coal and culm in the twelfth year of the reign of Queen Anne. There are also the bondsman's and the pilot's fee, the keelage and the hobblers' fees; expenses for labour and lighting, and of course, for ale, the cost of which often equalled the wages of the consumer. The purchase of an hourglass is recorded: while clocks had now found their way on board naval and larger merchant ships, they were by no means in common use on the smaller coasting craft.

Captain Richards' 'Bill of Expenses' for a cargo of culm taken to Tenby on 12 July came to £12.15s.6½d., itemised as follows (verbatim):

	£	s	d
To Mutton, 14 lb. at 4d. per lb. ...	0	4	8
To Bread ...	0	1	0
To Cheeze ...	0	1	2
To Potatoes ...	0	0	3 ½
To 3 Way, I Cart of Culm at 52s. ...	8	0	4
To 2 Carts of Coal at £6.2s.6d ...	1	0	5
To Collyers Wages ...	0	5	10
To Collyers and Shifters Ale ...	0	5	6
To help out of Minehead ...	0	1	6
To a Pilot on and of the Shore ...	0	5	0
To Clearing the Custom House ...	0	16	0
To the Land Waiter ...	0	1	0
To Help into Minehead ...	0	1	6
To 1 Hour glass ...	0	0	8
To the Warrant ...	0	0	6
To the Officers Ale ...	0	15	0
To Distcharging Ballisting Ale ...	0	7	0
To the Mans Wages ...	0	15	0
To the Boys Wages ...	0	4	0
To Beare ...	0	1	6
To 4 Mens Deners at 4d. Each ...	0	1	4
To 2 Shovel Sticks ...	0	0	4
	12	15	6 ½
To cash received ...	11	11	0
Ballce due to Rd Richards ...	1	4	6 ½

Sailing from Minehead on 12 July, Captain Richards had completed loading his cargo at Saundersfoot by the 14th, as appears by a receipt from the colliery:

1785. July 14ᵗʰ. Sheeped at Saundersfoot from Murton Colliery on Board the Industry of Minehead.

		£	s	d
To 3 1 of Culm at 52*s*.	...	8	0	4
To 0 2 of Cole at £2.2*s*.6*d*.	...	1	0	5
To Collers Wages	...	0	5	10
To Coller and Carters Ale	...	0	5	6
		9	12	1

The 'Master's Entry' on the Bond certificate was made up on 18 July, probably on the smack's return to the harbour, while the cargo was declared discharged by the 'Sworn Meter', Richard Martin, at Minehead on 19 July. So the whole voyage to Saundersfoot and back, including unloading, took from 12-19 July.

Voyages in the Bristol Channel at this period paid a fairly constant scale of wages, depending on their length and duration. To some extent these depended on the master of the vessel. An owner-master might pay a little more after a particularly profitable trip. In the majority of cases, however, the standard rate was adhered to. In this case Captain Richards, in running the vessel for Mr Luttrell, had a limited amount of cash in hand, and could not afford to be careless. In comparing the rates paid in the *Industry* with those paid in a similar smack of the same period, the rates are almost identical.

The above voyage paid at a slightly higher rate than usual for the run to the Welsh coast, probably because this voyage was a longer one — the man's wage being fifteen shillings and the boy's four shillings. A voyage to Aberthaw in the same vessel, and from 5ᵗʰ to 10ᵗʰ July, paid the man the more usual rate of eight shillings and the boy three shillings. A much shorter voyage to Aberthaw, from 20ᵗʰ to 22ⁿᵈ July, also paid the man eight shillings but the boy only two shillings. The following year a voyage to 'Brickcey Bay' on the Welsh coast, from 1ˢᵗ to 5ᵗʰ May, paid the standard wage of eight shillings to the man and three shillings for the boy.

At the close of the century the wages for a local trip from Minehead to Blue Anchor (about five miles) and back were surprisingly similar:

Account of two voyages to Bradley Gate for gravel for the repairing of the New Quay:

		£	s	d
To wages for my selve and allowance	....	0	17	4
To wages for the man	...	0	16	0
To wages for the boy	...	0	8	0
To the run of the vessel	...	2	2	0
		4	3	4

It is interesting to compare these costs with a similar voyage in 1939. We can do this as vessels traded out of Minehead into the fifties. Items such as wages, loading and discharging costs, victualling and maintenance show how the scales have altered. We have, for instance, an account of a voyage to Brickcey Bay in 1786, sailing from Minehead on 1 May:

	£	s	d
To help out of Minehead	0	1	0
To 21 stone at 6d. per stone	0	10	6
To loading	0	11	0
To help of the Shore	0	1	0
To throwing out the Cargo	0	3	6
To loading again	0	7	0
To help out of Aberthaw	0	2	0
To help into Minehead	0	1	6
To Bread	0	1	0
To Beef	0	4	0
To the mans wages	0	8	0
To the boys Do.	0	3	0
To a Man distcharging	0	1	6
To Ale	0	2	0
To help up in the Bay	0	1	0
Kiledge at Aberthaw	0	0	4
Beare	0	1	0
	3	2	4

The whole voyage, excluding the price paid for the stone, totalled £2.11s. 10d., of which which 34s. were paid in wages for labour and the run of the vessel, 9s.6d for hobblers and harbour aid, and 8s. for victualling and ale. The wage bill was unusually high on this trip because the vessel was loaded and unloaded twice; we do not know the reason for this. On the previous voyage, the wages had totalled 25s.6d. plus 6d. for the hobblers, while victualling and ale cost 5s.6d.

Compare this with a voyage undertaken on 12 April 1939, from Minehead to Lydney in the Forest of Dean and back, which cost £6.13s.1½d. The wages paid amounted to £4.; hobblers and harbour aid and dues, to £1.12s.2½d.; victualling to 18s.5d. and incidental expenditure for a shovel to 2s.6d., a far cry from the 'shovel sticks at fourpence' of the eighteenth century. Hobblers' fees and harbour dues have risen out of proportion to wages, due mainly to the cost of fuel and maintenance of navigational aids. In the case of Minehead, the hobbling fee had increased tenfold since 1785, while the wages for a man on a voyage had increased only sixfold. At this time, a man's wage for the trip to the Welsh coast was £2.10s. plus food. This often included loading, trimming, and unloading. Fifty shillings does not sound much for unloading fifty tons of coal with a shovel!

In an account of a voyage from Sharpness to Porlock on 20 July 1939, Porlock harbour dues amounted to five shillings, with one pound paid to the hobblers. This was cheaper than the dues at Sharpness: £1.5s.8d., plus 'Tippers and dock aid' amounting to 7s.6d. These details for 1939 are taken from an account book kept by Captain Philip Stanley Rawle of Minehead when he was the master of the ketch *Emma Louise,* the last vessel to trade out of Minehead.

A book kept at the City Archives, Bristol, entitled 'Vessels arrived Coastwise', forms part of a record kept of vessels arriving at the city quays. Only this one volume remains. It is dated from 29 September 1789 to 28 November 1807. From 10 October 1791, however, only vessels of 60 tons and over are recorded, probably because vessels in that category were liable to a duty of 40s. payable to the Mayor. Fortunately the lists do give us two complete years in which to see the recorded trips of coastal craft from the ports in the Bristol Channel to the port of Bristol, regardless of their tonnage. The following are noted as outwards from Minehead (Porlock and Watchet included) from 5 October 1789 to 10 October 1791, broken into one-year sections:

Vessel	Master	Tons burden	Trips In year One	Trips in Year Two
Sociable Friends	Will Hole (Watchet)	43	8	5
Nancy	Fran Jenkins	45	5	1
Betsey	Peter Nethey	22	6	4
(Minehead)	John Cobby			
	Chas. Couch			
Betsey (Porlock)	John Perkins	22	0	2
Friends Increase	Fran Jenkins	47	5	4
	Thomas Jenkins (Watchet)			
Good Intent	John Hurley (Watchet)	65	1	1
Unity	Will Atwill/Sitwell	33	4	4
Prosper	Thomas Jenkins (Watchet)	53	5	2
Brittania	John Dobbin	12	1	0
Two Sisters	John Perkins (Porlock)	36	3	0
William & Mary	Henry Jones	40	1	2
Fanny	John Moore (Porlock)	30	1	0
Who could have Thought it	George Needs	12	2	0
Ann	William Crocker (Watchet)	40	0	3
Wilton	Thomas Tamplin	65	0	2

The total number of voyages taken each year was 42 and 30 respectively.

The cargoes taken to Bristol were grain, flour, malt, hides, some leather, timber, and in season, chemical wood and kelp. The return trips were made with domestic and manufactured goods, provisions and beer. Chemical wood was the term given locally to green oak, cut early in May from the scrub oak of the Exmoor coast. Culbone and Embelle woods were important areas to the industry, which, in the early years of the nineteenth century, employed twenty to thirty men. The wood was cut and stripped of its bark, then shipped to Bristol or Swansea, where methyl-alcohol was obtained by destructive distilling. The end product was used in the production of methylated spirits. Bark was used in the tanning industry.

Kelp was shipped in large quantities in the 1790s from Watchet to Bristol, where it was used to produce potash for use in the glass industry. It is likely that the trips to Bristol by the larger craft from Watchet in those years were for this purpose. Cargoes across the Channel to Wales, principally to the ports of Tenby, Swansea, Aberthaw, Barry, Cardiff and Newport, were of flour, malt and timber, loading back with coal, culm and limestone. In many cases, the vessels were employed solely in the limestone, coal and culm trade, crossing to Wales simply with ballast.

Running out of Minehead in the eighteenth century contemporary with the *Industry* were several craft whose masters were listed as being prosecuted for the non-return of Coast Bonds: *Three Sisters* (Walt Crouch), *Loves Increase* (Chas Weston), *Bristol Packet* (Edward Court), *Ebenezer* (John Richards), *George & Thomas* (Tho Giles) and *Two Sisters* (Peter Martin).

As for the *Industry* herself, she appears to have retired from service in about 1791 and left to end her days in Minehead's 'Haven' for retired vessels. This was a slight depression beyond the shingle ridge at the point where the Bratton Stream now runs beneath the Promenade. Such ships were also broken up on the beach. By 1870, only one or two vessels remained there and after the arrival of the railway in 1874, the hulks of several small fishing and oyster-dredging smacks could be seen lying on the shingle bank itself.

One of the largest graveyards on this coast was at Porlock Weir, where some twenty hulks were harboured in the latter years of the nineteenth century. Not all were destined to remain as hulks, for in 1894 Captain H. J. Pulsford of Quay Street would buy one of these vessels: the *Ranger*, a smack of twenty-four tons, built in 1797. She had been bought by Mr John Ridd of Broomstreet Farm near Porlock some years earlier for use in his coal and limestone concerns. Captain Pulsford liked the look of the *Ranger*, bought and re-rigged her, and put her to work in the Bristol trade. When her master, Captain W. Slade, was asked about her condition in 1907, he replied that she was still an excellent little craft.

The *Industry* herself was made seaworthy again in May 1799, when Mr Luttrell, short of vessels to carry stone and gravel for the repair of

Minehead Quay, ordered her to be taken out of the Haven, repaired and re-rigged. The progress of this refit is recorded in several receipts for that year, for example:

May 21st 1799: 'To several charges of extra labour in getting the Old Sloop out of the Haven ... 3s. 6d.' [The work had continued the following day.] June 1799: 'John Fowles Luttrell Esq. To John James and Thomas Chapman To six days work each rigging the Sloop *Industry* for the use in repairing the New Quay at 4 shillings per day ... £1.4s.0d.'

From 1 July the *Industry* was once again at sea, bringing stone from Culvercliffe and Blue Anchor to Minehead. Four men went with her to help load and discharge her under the command of Thomas Chapman. They made eleven trips in all between 1 July and 27 September: nine trips to 'Culverclift and Greenaley', about half a mile west of the harbour, at 15s. per trip, and two trips to 'Bradley Gate', about five miles to the east of the harbour, at £1 per trip.

However, on 27 September 1799, the *Industry* loaded a cargo of stone near Greenaleigh Point, and soon after getting under way, was hit by a severe squall. Despite the efforts of the crew, she was driven ashore near Culvercliffe. All efforts to get her off failed, not helped by the swiftly ebbing tide. The age of her timbers, the weight of the stone in her hold and the rugged nature of the shore combined to damage the ship beyond repair. Word was quickly brought to the masons working on the quay; they laid down their tools and hurried across the beach to discharge her, while her master Thomas Chapman and two other men set about removing the sails and rigging:

'Sept. 27th, 28th, 29th July 1799. John Fownes Luttrell Esq. To Thomas Chapman Dr. For three days and two nights, myself, John Hensley and William Reed working on the saving of the seals riging etc. Of the Sloop Industry when drove ashore at Greenaly ... £1.7s.6d.'

With October, the weather deteriorated and the vessel was further damaged. The position of the wreck also made it difficult to work on her for long periods due to the tide cutting off the approach from the beach. An unsuccessful attempt was made on 25 October to salvage some of the heavy gear. Nothing more is heard of her until 25 July the following year, when the following account was delivered to Mr Luttrell: 'To six men and a boat in going down to Greenaley for the Mast Bowsprit Boom Gaff and Anchor of the Sloop Industry drove on shore there and placing it away in the Quay Court ... £0.17s.0d.'

Many sloops were centenarians, among them the *Looe* (built 1787), the *Ceres* (1811) and the *Ranger* (1797), all of which survived well into the nineteen hundreds, the *Ceres* until 1936. It is not unlikely that the sloop *Industry* was among their number, as a vessel with this name is mentioned in the records of the merchant William Alloway of Minehead as belonging to that port in 1687. So we may have been following the later history of a vessel that was, at the time it was wrecked, at least 112 years old.

During the years 1785–1791, all the repairs done on the *Industry* were undertaken by Thomas Manston's yard. This shipyard, situated immediately behind the harbour, comprised all the area between the back of the cottages once there, the harbour wall and the beach: some 16,000 square feet in all, with a frontage of about 260 feet. The advantage of this situation, later adopted by the lifeboat, was due to the steepness of the shingle beach, thanks to the longshore drift from west to east. Here the tide did not recede as far as it did — and still does — in Minehead Bay, so deep water was not absent for long periods. Consequently the yard could receive vessels at various stages of the tide, and was in a position to launch more easily too.

The first record of the yard itself is found in a plan of the harbour dated 1701, when about 850 tons of shipping was registered as belonging to the port. Throughout the last decades of the seventeenth century, Minehead's trade was booming. In 1680, for instance, 32 outward and 294 inward shipments were recorded. It is very probable that the yard owed its origin to this extremely busy period. The last vessel of which we have record as being launched there was the sloop *Unanimity* in 1798; the next vessel we know of that was built at Minehead — and the last — was built and launched 600 yards to the east, well up in the bay, near the junction of Blenheim Road and the Promenade. A tops'l schooner named the *Perriton*, she was launched in 1881.

A photograph of the site of Manston's yard taken in about 1870 shows a roadway leading through the area. There appear to be the remains of a slipway marked by a worn patch and a shallow depression in the shingle about fifty yards to the west of the present Lifeboat House. Other than this, nothing remained of this once flourishing shipyard.

Thomas Manston's irregularly-kept account for the repairs of the *Industry* for the years 1785-87 also include the everyday items needed in a little country shipyard: scrub oak brought from the Culbone woods (very tough wood from the low-growing oak trees exposed to the westerlies, for tree-nails), furze for general fuel and to fire the steam boxes in which planks were bent into shape; iron nuts and bolts brought from Bristol in the sloop *Packet*:

> *1785. John Fownes Luttrell Esq. D^r to Thos. Manston for work doon and stuf used on the Sloope Industrey from Augst 8 1785 to Sept. 3rd 1787.*

			£	s	d
Augest 8					
To 1 lb. of Oakm ...	at 2d.	...	0	0	2
To 3 lb. of Pich ...	at 2d.	...	0	0	6
To 3 lb. of Nails ...	at 4d.	...	0	1	0
To 2 Boalts 3 ½ lb. ...	at 4d.	...	0	1	1
To 1½ days work William Portman	at 2'6	...	0	3	9
Sept 10th					
To 2 Brums ...	at 1½d.	...	0	0	3
20th					
To 1 quart Ale John Sully on Board	at 4d.	...	0	0	4
28th					
To ½ a hundred of Nails ...	at 8d.	...	0	0	4
Novmb 10th					
To 1 lb. of Nails ...	at 4d.	...	0	0	4
To ¾ days Work ...	at 3'	...	0	2	3
Dec 19th					
To ½ hundred of Nails ...	at 2'	...	0	1	0
To 5 foot of 1 ½ Inch Oak	at 4½ d.	...	0	1	10 ½
To 6 Trunnels ...	at ½ d.	...	0	0	3
To 1 ½ days work	at 3'	...	0	4	6
27th					
To 1 days work ...	at 3'	...	0	3	0

In 1786, on 4 February, '6½ foot anker stock' at one shilling a foot cost 6s.6d. On 17 March, besides the cost of one day's work at the usual rate, '8 fackets [*sic*] of furse' cost 6d.; '3½ foot of 1½ Inch Oak' cost 1s.3¾d.; 3 lb of pitch cost 6d, and 2 lb. of 'Oakm' cost 4d. One day's work was also claimed for 17 April, when the purchase of 2 foot of 3-inch Oak, another 3 lb of pitch, and two different lots of nails: 'a quarter of a hundred' at 2s. a hundred and the same amount at 8d. a hundred, costing 6d. and 2d. respectively, were noted. On 12 May, two brooms at a penny-half-penny each, along with two 'fackets of furse' for a penny half-penny, joined the usual list of 'Oakm', pitch and nails (1 lb for 4d.), with ninepence for a quarter of a day's work. Two more 'fackets of furse' were listed on 30 May, along with the usual nails (twenty-five each of both kinds), pitch (4 lb), and '16½ of tare' for 2s.9d. The purchase of 1 lb of nails for 4d. on 3 June brought the total so far spent to £2.13s.11¼d.

Work continued on the *Industry*, with similar amounts of nails, pitch and 'Oakm' being noted, along with the names of some of the workers:

July 18th				£	s	d.
To 6 lb. of Pich	....	at 2d.	....	0	1	0
To ¾ days work George Summers	at 3'		...	0	2	3
To ¼ days work Thos Baggs	....	at 3'	...	0	0	9

August 2nd						
To 2 pleats	...	at 6d.	...	0	1	0

31st						
To 3 lb. of Pich	...	at 2d.	...	0	0	6
To 1 lb. of Oakm	...	at 2d.	...	0	0	2

Oct 9						
To ½ days work	...	at 3'	...	0	1	6
To 4 lb. of Oakm	...	at 2d.	...	0	0	8
To 3 lb. of Pich	...	at 2d.	...	0	0	6
To 3 lb. of Nails	...	at 4d.	...	0	1	0
Oct 9 [cont.]						
To 3 foot of 2 Inch Elm	...	at 6d.	...	0	1	6
To 2 days Work Jenkins	...	at 3'		0	6	0
To Blocking etc.	...	at 8d.	...	0	0	8
To 1 foot of 2 Inch Oak	...	at 6d.	...	0	0	6

Novmb 3rd					
To repairing a ladder and Trunnels at 1'	....	0	1	0

In 1787, a man and a boy worked half a day each on 28 January. The boy got fourpence halfpenny. William Portman did a quarter of a day's work on 21 February, at the usual rate; 1½ lbs of 'Nails The Shew' at 4d. a pound were also bought that day. William Portman worked a day and a half on 4 May, earning 4s.6d. Three pounds of 'Oakm'; nine pounds of pitch and half a pint of oil for 3d. were also listed, while 4d. was spent on 'Blocking'. On 9 May, besides 2s.3d. for three-quarters of a day's work, a pair of oars for the boat were purchased for 4s.

Pitch and oakum continued to be bought, on 18 July, 11 August, 22 August and 3 September, the last day of work. Nails at different prices figured in the accounts too: 25 for 2d. in July; 150 for 9d. and 25 for 6d. on 11 August 11. On the same day were noted:

To 3 foot of Elm board	...	at 1¾ d.	...	0	0	5½
To 5 Boat timbers	...	at 4d.	...	0	1	8
To 4 foot of 1½ Inch Oak a gunnell	at 4½ d.	....	0	1	6
To 4 days work	...	at 3s.	...	0	12	0

Two 'fackets of furze' for a penny-halfpenny and half a day's work were also noted for 22 August, while three-quarters of a day's work was noted for 3 September. The total received on 26 October 1787 by Thomas Manston from Mr Luttrell's agent William Gale for doing the repairs was £5.12s.4¾d.

Another sloop, the *Unanimity*, was launched from Manston's yard in May 1798. Thanks to a duplicate certificate of registry made out in 1803, we know her dimensions. Officially designated a square-sterned sloop, she was 38 foot long with a beam of 14 foot. Her registered tonnage was $33^{44}/_{97}$. She was deep in draught for her size as the depth in her hold was 7ft.4in.

By comparison, the tops'l schooner *Florence Muspratt* of 78 tons and 80 foot long had a depth in hold of 10ft.5in. Though built at the end of the century, she carried the stamp of the middle of the century, being bluff-bowed, beamy and stoutly timbered. *Dolphin*, *Looe* and *Ranger* of Porlock and Minehead are examples of this build. Excellent sea boats, they proved themselves again and again in the Bristol Channel, their years alone a tribute to their builders.

The *Unanimity* was bought on 7 May 1798 by John Fownes Luttrell for the sum of £106.10s.9¾d. Her first certificate of registry was made out on 28 July 1798, with James Crockford named as her master.

Acc of a voyage to Culver Clifte in the Unanimity for stones for the New Quay. 10th June 1799

To wages for my selve	...	0	7	0
To wages for the Boy	...	0	4	0
To wages for the Man	...	0	7	0
To the run of the vessel	...	1	1	0
		1	19	0

Settled the above ... Jas Crockford

By 2 August 1803, the *Unanimity* was re-registered as being under the ownership of James Crockford, with John Bushin mentioned as the master. Though Crockford was responsible for settling all voyage accounts and the vessel was ostensibly his, things were not as they seemed. For by a Bill of Sale dated 26 February 1820, Mr Luttrell's son John assumed ownership 'for and in consideration of the sum of five shillings and divers other good causes and considerations'.

There are many possibilities as to what may have happened. Perhaps the vessel, though registered and trading under the name of James Crockford for the period 1803–20, was still owned by the Luttrell family and reverted after 1820 to Mr Luttrell's son John Fownes some time after his father's death in 1816. Or Mr Luttrell may have sold or leased the vessel to Crockford (though no documents relating to such a transaction have been found), and its subsequent resale to the Luttrell family was due to some clause in the bargain or to the termination of the lease. There are many other possible reasons but what actually took place may never be known. At this point the *Unanimity* sails out of all local records and most likely ended her days laid up in the Haven.

During the second half of the eighteenth century, trade gradually declined. In a list of all the craft under the administration of the Custom House at Minehead in 1790, only twelve vessels were listed for Minehead, of which only the first three still traded with Ireland:

Vessel	Master
Whitworth	Robert Franks
Britannia	William Tomkins
Effort	Phil Summers
Nancy	John Jenkins
Fair Trader	Richard Richards
Betsey	John Cobley
Rose	Will Cobley
Unity	Will Sitwell
Industry	James Crockford
Shepherdess	Will Bowden
Three Brothers	Thos Needs
Handy	Will Summers

There were also ten vessels listed for Watchet and three for Porlock. Twenty fishing vessels, most belonging to Minehead, were also listed. The listed vessels were most likely to have been smacks, with perhaps a larger ketch or two among them, for Thomas Manston records repairs to a 'keetch' in his accounts for 1785.

In the list, Captain Richard Richards is stated to be the master of a vessel called the *Fair Trader*, while James Crockford appears to be the master of the *Industry*. As no voyage accounts exist for 1789-1790, and all shipyard accounts ceased for the *Industry* on 5 January 1791, it seems certain that Richards went to the *Fair Trader* some time before the *Industry* passed into retirement and James Crockford, who was to take the *Unanimity* in 1789, became her master until she was taken to the Haven.

The first decade of the nineteenth century saw a slow decline from the impetus given in the previous century. Although the figures from the 1813 survey of the Port of Minehead seem healthy enough, averaging 211 shipments over the years 1810-1812, the position was far from encouraging. These are the figures for the 1813 Survey of the Port of Minehead:

Year		1810	1811	1812
Foreign Trade	In	14	36	46
Ireland	Out	6	2	3
Coasting	In	54	55	49
Coasting	Out	121	124	112
Coal shipments discharged at				
Minehead		74	73	73
Watchet		120	120	120
Porlock		16	19	18
Total		210	212	211

Savage, writing in 1830, gives only six vessels trading from the port, two in the Bristol trade and the rest trading to Wales. Grain, malt, bark, timber, flour and some leather were taken to Bristol, returning with iron and groceries. At the time of the 1832 Reform Bill, amongst their (unsuccessful) arguments for keeping Minehead a parliamentary borough, John Fownes Luttrell and his agent claimed that the harbour could contain up to six vessels of 400 tons, besides forty or so smaller ships, while ships of any size could ride comfortably in the roadstead. He stated that Minehead possessed the most secure harbour on the English side of the Bristol Channel; was well-sited for trade with Ireland, 'with which it does at present carry on some', and added hopefully that it 'might maintain a trade with the West Indies'. Those days were gone, however.

Yet by 1840 the pendulum was beginning to swing back again for Minehead with an increase in small-scale local trade by sea. Ship-building in the area now recommenced. The smack *John & William* was built at Porlock Weir in 1858; *Friends* was bought at about the same time; *Providence* was a regular trader to Bristol along with the speedy *Jane & Susan*, which in June 1861 would break all records by making the trip in 4 hours, 48 minutes without the aid of steam up the River Avon!

While larger schooners and ketches at this time were much in use, smacks like the veteran *Looe*, built in Cornwall in 1787, still had an advantage in being able to land cargoes on beaches where to risk beaching a larger craft would be foolhardy. Many smacks, however, were altered to become ketches. This not only increased their cargo capacity, if they had been lengthened, but also made them speedier and easier to handle. The *Elizabeth Anne* of Porlock, for instance, whose boom alone was equal to the length of some smaller smacks, left Minehead one morning with a cargo of bricks for Newquay, discharged her cargo there and was back in Minehead on the third day.

A record trip of another kind was made by a Minehead vessel returning from Bristol with casks of beer on board. Unable to enter Minehead harbour due to an ebb tide, the thirsty crew bored a small hole in one of the casks ... When the vessel did not come in on the succeeding tide but remained swinging at anchor in the bay, those on shore began to feel anxious, as much for the cargo as for the sailors: the vessel was towed in.

The arrival of the railway in Minehead in 1874 hastened the decline of the trading smack. Hancock lists only ten such vessels, apart from small fishing boats, belonging to Minehead in 1901. T.K.Ridler owned not only the *Looe,* the *Susannah,* the *John & William* and the *Orestes,* but also the pride of his fleet, the schooner *Perriton;* the *Destiny* belonged to E.A. Pulsford and the *Ranger* to H.J.Pulsford. John Webber owned the *Harriet Ann* and W.J.Webber, the *M & E.* There were also Martin and Hole's *Mary Ann,* E.J.Perkins's schooner *Flying Foam* and J.B. Marley's *Thistle.*

At the end of the nineteenth century a host of large fishing smacks still crowded Minehead harbour, and in cases where visiting craft were wind-bound, there was no room at all for even the smallest vessels.

> *Lively, Lion* and the *Lark,*
> *Tom Bowline* and the *Shark,*
> The *Why Not* and the *Bucky Blue,*
> *Who'd a' Thought It, What Say You.*

This verse was composed to help the youngsters of Minehead in the early years of the twentieth century remember the names of some of these local boats. The colourful names of many of the above craft are real enough; the recorded trips to Bristol of the *Who Could Have Thought It* look most incongruous among the hundreds of more dignified names.

The one job the railway could not do more speedily than these smacks was to transport coal from South Wales. It was in this task that the last smack, and eventually the last vessel to trade out of Minehead, was employed. An unhappy chapter could be written about the period 1875-1910, for by the end of this period a dozen or more smacks lay rotting in the 'graveyard' at Porlock Weir. Some, like the *Ranger,* emerged to a new life; others remained, grotesque monuments to a passing era. In 1912 the graveyard was cleared and with it went the *Sophia,* the *R.J.W,* the *Ellen and Mary* and the *Samuel.* The *M & E.* lies today in the mud below Haverfordwest. The remains of countless others lie in the estuaries and mud-drenched tidal creeks of the Bristol Channel.

1. Watercolour painting of Minehead Harbour, c.1820s.

2. Earliest-known painting of Quay Town. c. 1725. Originally hung in Dunster Castle, it was given to Minehead Urban District Council in 1951, when Geoffrey Luttrell handed over the harbour on a 999-year lease.

The prospect of Minehead-Bay from Canagres near Dunster exactly Delineated by Geo: Ward 1735:

Comp:ss   3 Part of Middle Town   5 The Bank   10 Warren-house
1 the Church   4 The Lower Town   6 Blackmore   11 Wales
                                                      7 The Key
                                                      8 The Marshes

3. George Woods' annotated drawing, 1735.

4a. Sketch by Margaret Froude Hancock, July 1884.

4b. Sketch of Minehead harbour 1827.

5. Windbound smacks in Minehead harbour 1874.

6a. Polacca brigantine alongside the quay and the 'gallows crane', c.1850.

6b. Trading smacks in the harbour, early 1880s.

7. Photograph by James Date, 1875, of North Hill and Quay Town.

8. Quay Town and North Hill from the beach, painted by Isabella Silver in 1880.

9. Beach House, Quay Street, before its demolition and the building of the new sea wall. Painted by Harry Frier in the late 1890s.

10. Minehead harbour in 1888. The three-story building is the 17th-century Customs House, demolished with other buildings when the pier was built. Only St Peters-on-the Quay (with the sliding door) and T.K.Ridler's coal store remain.

15. The Pier from above photographed between the wars, also showing the Lifeboat House and Ridler's coal store.

16a & b. Above & right:
Quay West: the gas works.

16c. Below:
Westbury Cottages, built above the old
lime kilns and demolished in the 1950s.

17a. Miss Rose Wills' photograph of herself and other Quay Town children in 1902. From left: Bill James, Tom Heard, Rose Wills carrying Jack Wills, Lucille Martin, Jack Martin, Dolly Burnett, Elizabeth Martin, Harry Wills, Jackie Wills, Ted Collins (behind) and Harry Chapman.

17b. from left: John Martin, Joan Slade, Lewis Slade and Jack Hickey with the 'Baby Hobby Horse' in the eary 1930s. Muriel Martin is inside the horse.

18. Clement Kille's photograph of Minehead harbour in 1912, showing the ketches *Thistle*, *Orestes* and *Susannah*. T.K.Ridler's little yacht *Triton* lies to port of the *Thistle*.

Clement Kille.

Minehead Harbour, 1912

19. The *Harriet Ann* and a visiting schooner in Minehead harbour at the turn of the twentieth century.

20a. The launch of the *George Leicester*, Minehead's first lifeboat, in 1902. The fallen man on the left has lost his balance after pulling away one of the skids used for launching.

20b. Members of Minehead's thriving model yacht club pose in front of the Pier Hotel before the First World War. Racing took place in the harbour.

21. Jim Martin's boat, 1927, photographed by Clement Kille.

22a. Mrs Fred Harrison with locals, officials and steamer crew at the entrance to the pier in the mid-thirties. Harry Hole, proprietor of the Pier Hotel, is second from the left; Captain Smith stands second from the right.

22b. Quay Street in the early twentieth century, after the houses, etc. on the seaward side had been cleared away to make the new Sea Walk.

23. The schooner *Mary Jones* visiting the harbour in the late 1920s. *Orestes* lies astern of her; the steamer *Wheatsheaf* lies alongside the Quay.

24. The *Arthur Lionel*, the last pulling and sailing lifeboat, is in the background as the new motorised lifeboat, the *Kate Greatorex*, prepares to launch in 1939.

25. Lifeboatmen posing with the *Kate Greatorex* in 1939 include, from the left, Coxswain John Slade, Jim Martin, Jim Slade, Harold Bushen and Alfie Webber.

26a. The Sailors' Horse outside the Pier Hotel in 1939, photographed by Alfred Vowles. The Western National bus driver and conductor are in the crowd.

26b. The Sailors' Horse in town in the late Forties, photographed by R. Kingsley Tayler. Left to right: Dorothy Binding, Gladys Webber, Alfie Webber (drums), Jack Webber (accordion), John Lazerus, Tony Milton, Edna Prescott, Iris Webber, Trevor Pope, Kathleen Thresher, Rose Prescott, Irene Sully, unknown boy, Christine Greenman from the Carlton Hotel and Mary Tame.

27. Quay Town seamen, early 1930s. From the left, Edwin Bushen (standing), Philip Stanley Rawle ('Old Stan'), Bill Slade, Harold Bushen, Jimmy Heard, Frank Rawle, William Henry Martin (Bill).

Left:
28a. The *Emma Louise* about to load pit props in 1932.

Below:
28b. John Slade in his motor boat *Mouette* with a sea cadet, c. 1938.

29. The *Emma Louise* in Minehead harbour.

30a. Sketch of a WW2 tanker of a similar class to the *Inverdargle*, sunk in the Bristol Channel. John Legge, independent war artist.

30b. Harbour defences in the Second World War.

31a. Thomas Hamson Rawle (1867-1954) in a photographic portrait commissioned by Minehead RAOB Lodge to celebrate his 77th birthday.

31b. Thomas H. Rawle's wife Margaret, née Tudball (1873-1925).

32. Minehead boats decked with flags for a regatta before World War Two.

Chapter Six: Minehead becomes a Seaside Resort

During the second half of the eighteenth century, the urge to travel — and the possibility of doing so in more comfort and safety than previously — was gaining ground with prosperous folk who wanted to experience for themselves the beauties of the West Country celebrated by Wordsworth, Coleridge and other Romantic poets. Road travel had greatly improved with the building of turnpikes and by 1799 a good road ran from Bristol to Minehead. By 1830, a coach already ran from the well-established *Plume of Feathers* to Bridgwater three days a week, returning on the alternate days. Mail coaches now also set off every day for Taunton from a new coaching inn, the *Wellington*. After 1844, visitors could also arrive by train, though they had to ride the last part, from Taunton station to Minehead, in a special coach. The railway reached Williton and Watchet in 1862, but would not reach Minehead itself for another twelve years.

In Minehead itself, a group of merchants had raised money in 1762 to build a road to the beach (the 'New Road', now known as Blenheim Road), running from Lower Town to the beginning of Quay Street. With Henry Fownes Luttrell's permission this road was quickly built; a toll house at the sea end collected money to repay the debt incurred.

The earliest visitors, willing to accept the hardships of poor roads, tended to be those who wished to explore Exmoor and its glories on horseback, by hired coach or on a walking tour. But visitors soon began to come to Minehead and Exmoor in larger numbers, not only for the peaceful atmosphere and beautiful countryside, but also for the sea-bathing which had become fashionable, especially after 1815. The contact with salt water was supposed to be good for one's health. Bathing machines pulled by horses were available for hire on the beach (people were also charged for using the beach). Once the person or persons (usually female) inside were suitably attired in their modest bathing costumes, the horse would walk backwards into the sea to a suitable depth, and the bathers would descend steps into the water. Men and boys could bathe from a more private beach at Warren Point.

'To a certain class who wish to visit the seaside,' wrote James Savage in 1830, 'Minehead offers many advantages; lodgings are low, provisions are good and cheap; there is a fine sandy beach, and they will not be annoyed by the company of the frivolous part of the fashionable world, of whom so many are to be found in some of our watering-places at particular seasons of the year'. Similar comments had been made in 1800 by a visiting vicar, the Rev. Richard Warner, who was likewise pleased that the distance from London and other large towns prevented 'those felicity hunters, the teasing insects of fashion' from disturbing those who preferred to enjoy nature in peace. Evidently our town has always been an attraction to more discerning folk, who come as much for the peace and beauty of the countryside as for the seaside. Pigot and Co's *National Commercial Directory* for 1830 stressed the beauty of the local scenery: 'a few miles to the westward the country is highly romantic and affords fine subjects for the pencil...'.

Visitor numbers apparently dropped during the Napoleonic Wars, but picked up again after 1815. According to Douglas J.Stevens in his booklet about the harbour guns, this was probably when the guns on the harbour were dismantled, especially as major repairs were again taking place, including a newly-constructed harbour head (financed by the then lord of the manor, John Fownes Luttrell). The guns were sunk muzzle down into the quayside to provide moorings for the smacks and ketches using the harbour. Two can still be seen there today.

The 1843 Tithe Map of Quay Street gives us an insight into Quay Town before the coming of the railway boosted visitor numbers and affected sea-going trade at the harbour. The accompanying document notes the rents payed to the Luttrells, who owned Quay Town including the harbour. The 1851 census gives additional information about the local residents. The inward side of Quay Street was then much as it is today, give or take a few buildings of later date, such as the pink house at the foot of the Zigzag Path. But the seaward side was quite different, being lined with buildings, yards and gardens, many on the site of the old wharfs, abandoned in the early seventeenth century when the present harbour was built.

At the foot of Blenheim Road was a large house known as Lamb Cottage, surrounded by its own sea wall. It was so-called after a disaster at sea in 1735, when the *Lamb*, a troop ship on its way to Ireland, was destroyed in a storm. Beyond Lamb Cottage, demolished in 1902, was a large gap giving access to the beach, where boats could discharge their cargo; then came a short terrace of cottages, then outbuildings and gardens. Some of the outhouses were used as smoke-houses for the herrings which were still caught from time to time, though rarely in such large numbers as previously. There were storehouses, coal cellars and coalyards which, like the gardens and barns, were mainly rented by residents of the houses opposite, built as these were tightly under the cliff of North Hill. Beyond the Quay, houses also existed on both sides of the road at Quay West; these were demolished when the gas holders were built, or even before. There were two inns by the harbour: the *Queen's Head* and the *Ship Inn.* Returning along Quay Street you would have found the *Hope and Anchor* at today's number 43, while the old thatched *Red Lion* was to be demolished and rebuilt in 1902. The Coastguard Cottages were not built until 1877.

In 1851 nearly all the inhabitants were connected with the sea and the harbour. Master mariners or ship-owners such as William Crockford and his family, William Morgan, Joseph Webber, John Bushen, the James families and Thomas Collins at Quay West, usually lived in the larger houses, while general seamen tended to live in small cottages along Quay Street and at Quay West. The women of the family were often listed in the 1851 census as dress-makers or sempstresses, and one was a milliner. The growing influx of visitors would be very advantageous for them. Many women, such as Jane Reed, Susanna Wicken and Sara Ann Dugdale lived on their own, sometimes renting much property. Such women were often wealthy widows or daughters.

On the Quay was the Luttrells' office, along with their two yards where spare ship parts were stored, such as the remains of the *Industry* as mentioned in Chapter Five. Next to the *Ship Inn* were the two storehouses ('cellars') formerly belonging to Robert Quirke, one of which is now St Peter's-on-the-Quay. Further along was the fine three-storeyed Customs House, dating back like the cellars to the early seventeenth century when the harbour was built. The Luttrells owned a shop near the Quay; two other shop-keepers were listed for Quay Town in the 1851 census. The wealthy William Hole gave his occupation as 'general merchant'. The ship agent, shipwright, carpenter, coal merchant, two masons and three labourers also had connections with the harbour. Thomas Collins had two stables, one at the Quay, one beside his large house at Quay West. This was still an era when horse power was the main means of conveying goods and people. There were at least two malthouses. James Crockford also rented a brewhouse on the seaward side of the street.

Such was Quay Town in the mid-nineteenth century: a self-contained, busy place relying mainly on the sea for employment. With the decline in trading and herring fishing, it would soon develop other means of livelihood, connected to holiday visitors and their needs. Pleasure rather than trade would become the *raison d'être* of the harbour. Beyond the harbour, Quay West would soon take on quite an industrial character.

The Luttrells owned most of Minehead as well as Quay Town. But with ownership came responsibility, and George Fownes Luttrell, who became lord of the manor in 1867, took his duties seriously. Both in Dunster and in Minehead, he deployed enormous energy and funds to bring both into the modern world. It is not surprising that Prebendary Hancock dedicated his history of Minehead, published in 1903, to G.F.Luttrell: 'to whose enlightened and unselfish policy Minehead owes in large measure her rapidly increasing prosperity'. However, self-interest was involved a little too. The decline in trade meant loss of revenue for the manor; poverty through loss of paid work meant unpaid rents, and any increase in the town's prosperity would also increase the wealth of the Luttrell family.

It was the Luttrell's agent Thomas Ponsford who successfully brought about the continuation of the railway, via Williton and Dunster, to Minehead. The family had been trying to bring the railway here from the 1840s, but it was not until 16 July 1874 that the trains finally reached the town. Streets were decorated with bunting and huge crowds greeted the arrival of the first trains.

Now Minehead began to prosper even more as a seaside resort, with visitors and day trippers able to arrive every day without respect to tides or the need for coaches. The muddy path to the beach beside Bratton Water had already been replaced by the present Avenue around 1869; the stream was taken underground. Gas lighting was installed in the town around the same time. A water company was formed in 1874 to provide piped water and in 1878 George Fownes Luttrell, at his own expense, built a network of sewers connecting most of the 300 existing houses in Minehead to mains drainage, with connections ready for the new houses it was planned to build. This must have eventually included Quay Street, judging by the applications made by some residents in 1901 to install indoor lavatories. The Minehead Electricity Supply Company would be installed at the foot of Quay Lane in 1903.

But even after 1874, many visitors still arrived and departed by sea, as they had before the roads were improved: the *Duke of Wellington* and the *Ranger* sailed every fortnight with cargo and passengers, while boats such as *Eliza*, *Friend* and *Blossom* crossed the Channel to Wales at irregular intervals. Channel steamers, too, would soon call regularly at Minehead, and Quay Town benefitted greatly from this influx of visitors. Rooms at the various sea-front inns had always been available for travellers. Now households in Quay Street began augmenting their income by offering lodgings 'with a sea view' or offering refreshments to day visitors.

A day trip to Wales or North Devon on one of the steamers calling at the harbour head when the tide was right was a big attraction for holiday-makers, who also arrived in their hundreds from Wales, especially on Sundays when the pubs there were closed. The *Lady Rodney* called as early as 1830. Later the *Defiance* brought train passengers on to Minehead from the railhead at Watchet. By 1874 its owner, R.S.Date, was also running excursions to Cardiff and Swansea. In 1886, some Bristol businessmen chartered a paddle steamer called the *Waverley* for the 1887 summer season. (The third of this name, built after the second was sunk in WW2, continued to visit Minehead in summer.) This venture was so successful that its owners, Peter and Alec Campbell, moved to Bristol from their base on the Clyde. Another paddle steamer, the *Ravenswood,* soon joined the Waverley and by the 1890s their newly-named White Funnel Fleet consisted of not two but seven ships steaming up and down the Channel from Bristol. Tickets could be bought at the Red Lion, where the tricolour Campbell's flag can be seen flying in an old picture at Townsend House. The problem for people wishing to board steamers at Minehead was that such large boats could only call at the harbour when the tide was in. This problem would be resolved at the beginning of the new century, with the building of a pier.

On disembarking, visitors coming to the town would have been able to enjoy refreshments in Quay Town or the town proper. Many chose to take a carriage ride up G.F.Luttrell's 'Marine Walk', cut into the north side of North Hill by 1857 and leading to Greenaleigh Farm, where they could partake of a cream tea or, as a special treat, junket. In the 1880s George Fownes also started laying out walks and carriage drives on the sunny side of North Hill. If visitors remained at the harbour, they could enjoy being rowed round the harbour, or spend a day fishing in the local sailing boats. All this provided useful additional income in Quay Town to replace what was lost through lack of trade. Enterprising residents also exploited the possibilities of the beach itself; one regular visitor in the nineties recalled that 'two very weather-faced Quay ladies ran the bathing huts and machines'. One of these may have been Elizabeth Webber, who was listed in the 1911 census as 'Bathing Machine Proprietor'.

Commercial fishing for herring, except in exceptional years such as 1895, was no longer profitable, so some local seamen had converted their fishing boats to carry cargo up and down the Channel or even closer to home. Others continued to fish inshore in the traditional ways and sell their catch on the quayside; more of this in the next chapter. Even those without a boat could catch fish in various ways. The old fish traps still visible at low tide, with their V-shaped formations, were still in use. They enclosed a knee-deep pool left by the receding tide in which fish might be trapped. Crowds would sometimes gather round at low tide to see the fish brought out and taken home in baskets.

The line of stakes still occasionally used on the beach opposite the Red Lion was in regular use during the herring season, the autumn. Nets were hung between the stakes, which form an S-shaped line at right angles to the shoreline. Another way of catching fish was to lay a baited fishing line, up to about sixty yards long, along a low gulley made by removing stones in a straight line, and reinforcing the sides with larger stones. These were especially used during the winter months to catch cod. They were visited day and night to remove fish and rebait the hooks; it was wise to be near your gulley as the tide went out, to prevent any unscrupulous person stealing 'your' fish.

Trade in the second half of the nineteenth century continued in a small way with eight or ten trading smacks. Besides the major imports and exports noted below, groceries continued to be brought to Minehead and other local harbours by sea. These included flour: Harry Baker's horse Prince figures in many photographs around the turn of the century as he waits on the quayside for his cart to be loaded. The job of unloading cargo was vied for by both men and women, women such as Quay Town resident Charlotte Morgan, who died in her nineties in 1929. Their pay was as much of the cargo as they could carry home. This must have been a great help to their families, especially as the lack of seamen's jobs locally meant the men were often away from home on vessels sailing from the larger ports. The 1861 census notes many 'sailor's wives' at home on their own.

The Quay Town community included rich as well as poor. Quay Town ship-owners listed in 1861 included John Dugdale the harbour master and William Hole. Apart from three inn-keepers, these were the only Quay Town residents to have a live-in servant, apart from wealthy widows Susan Crockford and Susanna Vicklen (or Wicken) and the Chief Coastguard Officer John Page. The latter actually had three servants: a cook, a housemaid and a nursemaid for his two children aged one and two. Other families in Quay Street had children listed as working as servants in other homes. One such was Sarah Sparkes, aged nineteen, whose contribution to the family income must have helped support the rest of her family: mother, father, three adult seamen, one mason's boy and eight younger children aged from 12 years to 10 months. This large family lived at Quay West in a cottage which disappeared long ago. Families with four or more children were not uncommon: the extra mouths to feed were balanced to some extent by the number of workers in the family once children had left school at twelve or, at the latest, fourteen.

There were still sailing ships gracing the harbour, especially when ketches and schooners were visiting or sheltering from bad weather. When local craft were moored alongside the quay, schooners and other visiting vessels had to tie up to one of the posts at the edge of the harbour. Limestone and culm ('slack', a soft, sooty coal for mixing with the lime to burn it), were the major imports, though coal was needed for the town tannery and coke would become important once the gasworks was built at Quay West in 1879. At the end of the century, bricks and tiles from J.B.Marley's new Victoria Brickworks at Alcombe were also exported from Minehead to Ireland, Cornwall and the south coast, in Marley's own vessel, the *Thistle,* and later in T.K.Ridler's *Orestes.*

Iron ore was exported to South Wales in small quantities around mid-century. There were various small iron mines around Minehead. The one near Brockwell sometimes had so much ore to export that teams of horses and even local people's donkeys were used to cart it to Minehead harbour. Sometimes over 200 tons were waiting on the quayside to be loaded. Binding and Stevens, in their *Minehead: a New History,* relate that in March 1854 one resident of Quay Street living near the *Red Lion,* complained to the lord of the manor because this traffic was shaking the house so much that 'gentlefolk', presumably holiday visitors, refused to lodge with him; other residents complained about the noise early in the morning. This activity did not last long: deposits were small and soon exhausted.

Local hardwood was exported by T.K.Ridler, whose timber and builders' yard just above the beach on North Road was prospering, partly due to all the new buildings being erected in town. He also shipped road metal for building the new roads. But T.K.Ridler combined keeping up with the times with his love of sail. He owned a fleet of vessels of which one, the schooner *Perriton*, built on the beach just below his yard, was the last vessel to be built in Minehead. It was launched in 1881.

Quay West was taking on quite an industrial aspect. In 1869, the Minehead Gas Light and Coke Company built their gas works conveniently close to the harbour, as it would run on imported Welsh coal. While excavating the shingle below the site for the main drain, part of a whale's spine was discovered, twelve feet below the surface. It belonged to the species *Hyperodon Rostratus*, rarely seen in British waters. This relic used to be preserved at Dunster Castle. A proper road had been built along Quay West in 1868 to accommodate the gas works, with two houses for the manager and foreman. Other houses would be built for workers in later years as the gas works expanded, including some above the former lime kilns in Quay West.

In 1887 T.K.Ridler, who had acquired the contract to import coal for the gas works, built a huge storehouse at the end of the wharf, for coal underneath and grain above. Having the coal storage so close to where the coal was unloaded made a lot of sense. The coal would be brought from South Wales in return for pit props and other cargo. Around 1886 a steam crane had replaced the ancient hand-operated crane known as Griff's Gallows, after Captain Griff Pulsford, who was renowned for the proprietorial attitude he had towards its use and maintenance. The crane moved on rails to where it was needed. Coal cargoes could now be discharged into large iron buckets on the quayside, instead of into baskets which had to be carried up a plank from the ship, a rather hazardous manoevre.

In 1872 Thomas Lomas, a chemical fertiliser manufacturer from Yorkshire, moved to Minehead and built two factories, one near the brick works on the Warren, which was closed in 1886, the other at the end of Culvercliffe. The Bristol Channel Chemical, Sulphuric Acid and Chemical Manure Works produced artificial fertiliser using an 8-horse-power steam engine. The necessary high chimney can be seen in the background of early photographs of the harbour. This factory, about 140ft long and 100ft wide, consisted of two storeys; it was made of stone pillars with board between them and had a tarred felt roof. Thomas Lomas and his family had a villa, *Clevelands*, built for them on the south-facing side of North Hill in 1877, after a failed attempt to build a house on the bare hillside above the works. Lomas had not realised that the springs he hoped to use for his water supply were unreliable, so the project was doomed. The partly-built house can still be seen beside one of the footpaths up North Hill from Culvercliffe. However, nothing is left of the Quay West factory, which was sold to a Mr Heller. On 25 October 1887 the furnace used to prepare the sulphuric acid and glue overheated and the whole building, apart from the chimney stack, burnt down. Now not even the chimney stack remains.

Away from Quay Town, Minehead was taking on its present character. New terraces sprang up during the 1880s, offering better housing for residents and more choice of holiday lettings for the visitors. The imposing terrace known as the Esplanade Buildings was erected in 1875, to be joined in 1893 by the Esplanade Family Hotel, for wealthier patrons. This prestigious hotel was renamed the Metropole Hotel five years later, and would be extended in 1912-13. Floyds, which would continue to play a role in Minehead life into the 1970s, was one of several department stores developed for the use and delight of visitors. New churches and chapels were built, such as St Andrews in Wellington Square and the Catholic Church in Townsend Road. Many of Minehead's finest buildings date to this period, including the Civic Centre designed by Piers St Aubyn (Minehead's hospital until 2011) which was completed in 1889. Minehead became first a Local Board District (significantly, its badge was of a sailing ship over a woolpack), and then in 1894, the Minehead Urban District Council.

At the end of the 1880s, the only prominent villa on the side of North Hill other than *Clevelands* had been the fortress-like *Elgin Tower* (1887). But as well-off people from other parts of Somerset, and increasingly, from elsewhere, began to see Minehead as a pleasant place to which to retire, plots were sold off by the Luttrells for new villas. J.L.W.Page, writing in 1890 in his book on Exmoor, complained that much of the old paved way from Quay Town to St Michael's church had been blocked by new roads and houses. During the second half of the nineteenth century, Minehead's population almost doubled.

All these visitors and new residents brought prosperity and the chance of employment: women and girls could become dressmakers, milliners, shop assistants or go into service in the large villas being built; boys and men were needed to construct and decorate the villas or to look after the numerous horses. (A church supper given by the vicar, the Rev. Etherington, and his wife in 1913 entertained nearly one hundred grooms and drivers.) Many visitors brought their own hunters or hacks, other horses were needed to draw carriages or coaches. There were eventually so many horses here during the season that a site for a further reservoir for Minehead's water supply had to be found. The 1881 census showed an increase in the number of Quay Town residents working as servants and labourers in building and agriculture if male, and as dressmakers, milliners or servants if female. The majority of heads of families were still listed as sailors or mariners, but again, many were away from home at the time the census was taken.

A popular institution from 1881 on was the annual 'Visitors' List' published by Cox's *Minehead & West Somerset Advertiser*. Besides acting as a town guide, this listed the summer visitors to town and noted where they were staying. Quay Street was a popular area in which to lodge. According to Bond's 1879 *Guide to Minehead and its Neighbourhood*, lodgings could be obtained at nearly all the houses at the Quay. In July

1887, visitors were staying at least ten cottages in Quay Street: Lamb Cottage ('reckoned the most commodious'), Beach House, Berkeley House, Bellevue House, Rock Cottage, Hardwick House, Sea-Cliff House, Seaside House, 1 Pier House and Rock View. Landladies and houses varied with the years, but until 1914 the numbers of houses offering lodgings were fairly stable. This was obviously a useful contribution to the family income, as was taking in washing from the hotels which had sprung up in the town.

Quay Town was no longer the largest of the three 'towns' of Minehead but it still had its own traditions and remained a close community. There was much intermarriage and everyone knew everyone else. This is still true even today, although many cottages have been sold or let as holiday homes. One tradition which continues is the Hobby Horse, which leaves its 'stable' near the harbour at dawn on 1st May and follows a set route through the town. For the next three days it can be seen in and around Minehead, accompanied by its Quay Town instrumentalists, usually drummers, accordionists and pipe-players, playing a traditional tune. (Vaughan Williams, with his interest in folk music, apparently made a musical arrangement of this tune.) The collections taken are for Minehead lifeboats. The growth of Minehead at the turn of the 19th century produced a rival in 1905, the Town Horse; other Horses appeared in later years; the rivalry between them all was fierce.

By the end of the century, trade had declined drastically: the timber trade was dying (but pit props would still be exported into the 1950s); there was little call now for 'chemical bark'. Ship-building and rope-making had declined along with the numbers of sailing vessels. Several Quay Town seamen still owned small coasters, such as Henry Pulsford's *Ranger*, W.J.Webber's *M & E*, and T.K.Ridler's *Looe*, *Perriton* and *Orestes*. But from now on, the harbour would be more associated with providing leisure facilities than with trade, though the gas works would continue to need imports of coal.

Queen Victoria's death in 1901 coincided with major changes at the Quay. Not only would a pier be built to the west of the harbour, so that pleasure steamers could call at any stage of the tide, but also most of the buildings associated with the seventeenth-century harbour would be swept away within a few years, though T.K.Ridler's new coal store survived, remaining in use well into the twentieth century.

Since there was no longer any need for the Customs House on the Quay, the customs offices were moved to 33 Quay Street, now known as the 'Old Custom House'. The 17th-century building was destroyed, along with various smaller buildings and the inner of Quirke's two cellars, known as 'the Gibraltar Cellars', to make way for the entrance to the new pier. The 'cellars' had been taken over by the parish in 1830 but fell into disrepair. The upper floor was briefly a Sailors' Home in 1888, a temperance shelter for sailors (an idea of George Fownes Luttrell's) but soon reverted to being a store. By 1898 the thatched roof had been tiled and a large sliding door installed. Because of the curse put on the cellars by Quirke, who had dedicated the rent in perpetuity to pay for the upkeep of his almshouses in the town, the outer store at least survived. In 1905 the vicar of Minehead, the Rev. F.M.Etherington, made it into a mission room for sailors and by 1907 the ground floor had been converted into a Sailors' Chapel, St Peter's-on-the-Quay, with a Reading Room above.

The *Ship Inn* was replaced by the newly-built *Pier Hotel* (since renamed the *Old Ship Aground*), proprietor Harry Hole, in 1900. This could offer such modern luxuries as 'hot and cold baths' as well as the 'good stabling and loose boxes for hunters' offered by all the major hotels. The wharf had to be extended in front of the Pier Hotel, right on the edge of the harbour, and the slipway also had to be rebuilt, but Pulsford's weighbridge at the head of the quay remained there until the 1930s.

The new pier was officially opened by George Fownes Luttrell on 1 June 1901 to great rejoicing. Made of a lattice of cast iron and steel, it was 250 yards long and jutted into the sea at right angles to the beach, behind and to the left of T.K.Ridler's storehouse. At low tides, some of the infrastructure can still be seen. The pier had two landing stages, so that visiting steamers could load and unload at low or high tide. A call at Minehead was now included in the regular timetables of the pleasure steamers, which put the town on a level with the leading seaside resorts of the Bristol Channel. Visitors arrived in their thousands; for those who did not or could not walk to the town, horse-buses or horse-drawn carriages were waiting at the end of the pier. This caused traffic jams in Quay Street, especially where the road had to squeeze between the Red Lion and the cottages opposite it at the town end of the street.

Campbells' steamers could now run daily in summer back and forth to Cardiff, as well as to North Devon several times a week. The Red Funnel Fleet, owned by the Barry and Bristol Steamship Company, whose tickets were sold by Captain Vickery from his cottage opposite the Red Lion, competed for a while but Campbells' White Funnel Fleet gained a monopoly. Their ticket agent was based at the Pier Hotel. The names of the steamers became well-known (several B & B's in Tregonwell and Glenmore Roads are named after them). The *Ravenswood* had special ties with Minehead and many lads from Quay Town found jobs on it or on other steamers, living on board. Older seamen might choose simply to work by day and return home for the night.

A stroll to the end of the pier (costing two pence) was recommended in the guide books as most bracing. So bracing, in fact, that in a few years shelters had to be built for passengers awaiting the ferry: a wide shelter halfway, and a kiosk on one side. Long-stay visitors as well as day-trippers used the steamers, so a little trolley line was built down the centre of the pier for their luggage. Tickets were checked at the smart entrance with its two kiosks.

Later in 1901 the fine Lifeboat House was built on land beside the pier donated by George F. Luttrell. Until then a boat dedicated to life-saving emergencies had been kept in the cottage nearby, which still exists. But the *Forrest Hall* disaster in January 1889, when, for lack of a proper lifeboat at Minehead, the Lynmouth lifeboat was famously dragged over the road to Porlock, made it clear that Minehead should have its own lifeboat. The *George Leicester*, a pulling and sailing boat, arrived the following year, paid for by a Miss Leicester from London. This was the first in a long line of ever-improved lifeboats and a proud tradition of service in them, celebrated in an exhibition in the Lifeboat House which is open in the summer season.

As Minehead grew, so did the demand for gas. In 1898 the works were completely rebuilt and a new gas holder erected. Two more were added in 1900. The increased traffic meant that the *New Inn,* built into the back of the hill opposite the *Pier Hotel*, had to be demolished. The *Queen's Head* had also disappeared by the end of the century, while the *Hope and Anchor* at number 43 had reverted to a private house. This left the *Red Lion Hotel* as the sole remaining public house in Quay Street. Opposite the entrance to the Quay, two large Victorian houses had replaced buildings shown on the 1843 tithe map.

Quay Street was still lined on the seaward side by gardens, outhouses and even houses at the town end. However, these were in poor shape, and more walls collapsed with every storm that drove the shingle up onto the gardens and flooded the buildings. The only protection from the sea was the residents' own walls. George F. Luttrell had begun to build a continuous sea wall along the top of the beach, starting from the beach end. Beside it he intended to provide a 'Sea Walk', connecting the Esplanade to the harbour, for the greater enjoyment of visitors. By 1901 the new sea wall was almost complete except for the Quay Street end. But the houses oposite the *Red Lion* were still lived in and Mrs Vickery was offering holiday lettings in the end cottage, *Beach House*, as late as 1904, even though the sea came in at the back and out at the front every gale-driven tide. After a particularly destructive storm in 1910, however, the inhabitants: the Vickerys, Brufords and Threshers, were re-housed elsewhere in Quay Street by the Luttrells. Their houses were knocked down to allow more room for the flow of visitors coming off the steamers and the passage of heavy traffic on its way to the gas works.

Destructive storms occurred quite often, notably in 1859 and 1901, but the storm in December 1910, known locally as the 'Great Gale', also smashed up most of the existing promenade, destroying shelters and beach defences. Quay West, too, was badly affected: the gasworks, only separated from the sea by a narrow road much worn by waves, felt the full force of the gale. The sea burst open the yard gates and flooded the yard. The manager's house, the office and several nearby cottages were also flooded. Quay Street homes were also flooded in March 1912, after a night of bad weather raised the sea level several feet above normal.

By 1914, Minehead was a flourishing seaside resort, with all the expected Edwardian attractions: a beach with bathing machines and beach huts (owned by the hotels; the first private one to be rented from the Luttrells was allowed in 1905); donkey rides on the sands; a bandstand; visiting entertainers (the Queen's Hall was built in 1914); excursions into the countryside; cream teas; tennis courts, and pleasant walks up North Hill. Societies of all kinds flourished, including a Choral Society. Horse races, which drew large crowds, were held on the beach, where sand-yachting also took place. Polo was popular with spectators too: the horses could be watched exercising on the beach, where the matches were held too. The wealthy brought their own polo horses in by rail to play with the West Somerset Polo Club. The horses were taken off the train at Dunster station. Later polo was played on the Lawns at the foot of the castle meadows.

At the harbour, besides watching Quay Town workers load and unload the trading smacks, visitors could hire a rowing or sailing boat themselves, or be taken out pleasure-fishing on a local boat. The sight of ships in sail was also an attraction, especially if a schooner was visiting.

Horses and carriages were still the main means of getting about, along with tradesmen's carts for goods, but in 1908 the first motor car, owned by a visitor, arrived in the town. A motor coach which the same year offered excursions into the countryside met much opposition from local people, who feared to meet it on the narrow local roads. But by 1910, four local garages were offering motor char-a-banc trips, and most carriage works in the town had begun to offer to service motor cars. Minehead was easing itself into the twentieth century.

However, down at the Quay, it was as if the medieval feudal system still existed; the Luttrell family still owned Quay Town and the harbour as well as the foreshore where they continued to rent out the low-tide weirs to local fishermen. On more than one occasion, the squire and his friends hunted a stag right down through the town and into the sea: it would be up to one of the local seamen to row out to dispatch the doomed animal and tow it back to land. Rents were paid on the last Friday of the month, at the Luttrell office in town, the 'Old Priory' opposite the top of Blenheim Road. When 'the Squire' rode down Quay Street, the men would step off the pavement and doff their caps and women would curtsey. Was this genuine respect or fear of being thrown out of their houses, wonders a former resident? But the Luttrells were reckoned to be good landlords, rehousing families in need and allowing widows to stay in their homes even after the death of their husbands.

Certainly there were many in Quay Street who had no experience of any other life. After leaving school at twelve or so, they would get a job to contribute to their family's income, and often stay in it for the rest of their lives. To keep their self-respect, men would often develop characteristics to set themselves apart from others. This encouraged people to give them nicknames, which also helped to differentiate between different members of the same family. One of the Slades, James, lived in a boat drawn up onto the beach behind the harbour, and was known for some reason as 'Sam Can'. Another man grew his hair so long that it hung down his back. One evening he drunkenly boasted at the pub of how strong it was. Bending his knees while a heavy weight was tied to the end of his pigtail, he slowly stood erect and proudly turned round to face the crowd which had gathered. In response to their applause, he turned again and again, with disastrous results. The weight gained its own momentum, flying out to the danger of the bystanders and twisting his hair more and more tightly. Eventually, unable to stop, he spun out of control and crashed to the ground, losing much of his prized pigtail in the process.

Quite apart from the camaraderie of the pub, Quay Town residents made their own amusements. Captain James Vickery and Captain Lewis, who lived at 2, Blenheim Cottages, almost on the corner with Quay Street, were noted for singing sea shanties and folk songs, often with their own variations. Both died before the First World War but their songs were collected by Cecil Sharp. Entertainments given in the Sailors' Reading Room above St Peter's and elsewhere in the first decade or so of the twentieth century included contributions from Quay Street men such as William Roger Webber, who, with another Webber, sang and danced (including at least once, the hornpipe in nautical costume) at concerts.

The same William Webber is commemorated in St Peter's–on-the-Quay by a framed certificate and citation by the Carnegie Hero Fund Trust, for an act of bravery in August 1914, when he took a boat out with Walter Webber junior, and Thomas and Edward Heard, to save three bathers from drowning. Two were rescued and one lost. William Webber was given a medal and a certificate; the *Free Press* reported (6 February 1915) that he had been given £20; the other rescuers got £10 each.

The money must have been welcome, as although holiday visitors continued to make a contribution to the income of Quay Town residents, their picturesque cottages often concealed much hardship. Many families were large and it was a struggle to feed them. Clothes were handed down whether they fitted or not, including hobnail boots, which in one family at least were carried all the way to the Boys' Primary School in Watery Lane to save wear, and only then put on. Girls helped at home and wore a white pinny to protect their clothes. Bread and dripping was the usual breakfast, to last all day; small wonder that some Quay Town children would sometimes steal food from the better-off pupils at school. With jobs increasingly hard to find on the harbour with the decline in trade, many boys had to take work as labourers on local farms or in the town.

Next to the Red Lion, the coastguards had their own terrace with laundry rooms at the back, until the Admiralty sold their houses off in the 1920s. But most of the houses along Quay Street were dark, damp, frequently flooded and with little or no sanitation. At number 11a, for instance, there was at least an indoor lavatory, next to the scullery where the laundry was done by hand. Fish could be cleaned and gutted here, before being hung up on hooks on the wall outside (now the inner wall of Sashes' entrance hall) until someone came to buy them. Electric or gas lighting was too expensive for such homes, which relied on candles and oil lamps. In case of illness, doctors could only be afforded in extreme cases; otherwise parents relied on herbal remedies or a dose of castor oil. Thomas Hamson Rawle and his wife Margaret lived at number 11a from about 1912. They had two daughters and nine sons. The youngsters were fed in shifts from a huge iron cooking range: the three women fed the youngest first, then the older boys. When did they eat themselves? As for sleeping, the parents had the front room upstairs; the two daughters a tiny room at the back, while the nine boys slept in two double beds in a long, narrow third room, the three largest head to toe in one bed, and the younger ones as best they could in the other.

Quay Street women did whatever they could to contribute to the family income. Even if they had no lodgers, they could take in washing or do cleaning jobs in the guest-houses and hotels. Those clever with their fingers could make a living sewing or making hats for the summer visitors: several dressmakers and milliners lived in Quay Town. Other women found jobs in Minehead shops. Though the fishing was left to men, it was usually the women who had the patience to make the fishing nets, if they could find enough space somewhere to do so.

Most of the men were seamen and often away on vessels based in Watchet or elsewhere. But not everyone was strong enough to work on a sailing ship: hauling heavy sails and anchors about was physically demanding, and the ability to do it could mean the difference between life and death in one of the heavy storms that could blow up suddenly in the Channel. To maximise profits for the owner, the crew was kept to a minimum: usually captain, mate, cook (if the vessels were away overnight or longer) and a young but tough ship's boy. In Captain Thomas Hamson Rawle's family, eight of his nine boys went to sea: as they got older they progressed from being chef to mate to captain, mostly on T.K.Ridler's vessels. Philip Stanley ('Old Stan') would take over from his father as skipper of the *Orestes* at twenty years old.

However, the days of the sailing ship were numbered. The 1911 census showed that only eight men called themselves sailors, plus one who worked on a steamship, compared to over thirty in 1881. The main occupations given were as carpenters and masons (i.e builders), along with their apprentices. Labourers of various kinds: builders, bricklayers, painters and five farm labourers, were also numerous. Other Quay Street dwellers worked as errand boys and gardeners, or coal carters, while individuals included a crane driver, an oilman and a lime-burner. Only one person called himself a fisherman, though most men would fish for their families in their spare time. The gas works also employed at least five people.

So although many of these occupations might be concerned with the harbour and its vessels, very few men were actually engaged in working in sail, either from Minehead or further from home (some were merchant seamen). This does not mean that they would not go to sea, given the opportunity. Even Philip Stanley Rawle, who later sailed on many vessels including the *Emma Louise,* was a farm labourer in 1911, when he was sixteen, perhaps working for his uncles Philip and Stanley Rawle at Greenaleigh Farm. Many occupations, however, especially those of the women, who according to the census included dressmakers, domestic servants, laundresses, charwomen and one cook, were now connected with Minehead's new status as a seaside resort.

The Heard family, who lived at *Sea View,* in Quay West, is a good example of how old and new occupations could be found in the same family. The head of the family, Thomas Heard, aged 53 in 1911, was a sailor in the Merchant Service. He and his wife and their seven children shared the house with his newly-married daughter and son-in-law, Ed Jewell, who worked on an RN Torpedo boat. Thomas Heard's sons Thomas and Edward, however, worked at the Golf Club as clerk and groundsman respectively.

Apart from the merchant seamen, few men in Quay Town had travelled far from Minehead. Even Taunton seemed a foreign country. The coming World War would change all that, broadening horizons for those who returned.

Chapter Seven: World War One and the Interwar Years

The summer of 1914 was one of optimism. Seen from the perspective of seaborne commerce and experience among the ports of Europe and Scandinavia, the very idea of a war disrupting normal trade was unthinkable, especially to West Country seamen who felt a close comradeship with all European seafarers on a day-to-day basis. The Edwardian era, followed by the reign of George Vth from 1910, was one of increasing stability and order. War was not a welcome proposition for the coastal seamen and ship owners whose livelihood depended on international goodwill.

When war was declared it came as a shock. All Naval Reservists were immediately called up, including those who had only been attracted by the retainer. They were whisked away from their current vessels, often leaving these stranded with depleted crews. Any Quay Town men working on Campbell's steamers at the time remained with them, as most of the steamers were drafted into war work as minesweepers. However, local coastal seamen reckoned that their trading patterns would not be too adversely affected by what they saw as a clash of the battleships and battle cruisers massed in the two great fleets, and so they continued trading as usual.

In Minehead work continued extending the sea wall along Quay Street. A cargo of cement was due in August and it was hoped that the widening of Quay Street opposite the former *Red Lion* would be completed by the end of September. In the event, this was not completed until well after the end of the war. Campbells announced in 1915: 'There will be no steamers this season'; they would not return until 1919.

The harbour continued to work commercially. Still a port for the exchange of agricultural and domestic goods, Minehead imported coal, culm, limestone, fertilizer, gravel, tiles, manufactured goods and commodities; timber, farm produce, bricks and tiles, cattle and sheep, leather and scrap were exported. Looking across the harbour early in the twentieth century you would have seen J.B.Marley's ketch *Thistle* (lost in 1912), which delivered the bricks and tiles from Marley's factory to Ilfracombe, Padstow and on down the Channel as far as the South Coast. Other vessels using the harbour would have included the ketch *Orestes* belonging to T.K.Ridler, skippered by Captain Tom Hamson Rawle and used in Ridler's coal, timber and agricultural business, and perhaps T.K.Ridler's yacht, *Triton*, his ketch *Susannah* and his schooner *Perriton*, whose last skipper was Captain Joe Webber. Then there were the little trading smacks like the *M&E* and the nineteen-ton *Harriet Ann,* both owned by Jesse and Walter Webber. These were able to load small cargoes of up to twenty or thirty tons and discharge right up onto the beach, from where it would be collected at low tide by horses and carts. Shipping coal on down the coast to Porlock Weir or delivering to remote beaches like Glenthorne was just the job for these intrepid craft, which also brought the groceries and other small items from Bristol. The schooners and ketches of sixty to a hundred tons could go as far as Ireland, but the once-famous Atlantic fishing fleet had dwindled to just a few vessels by 1914; the boats were either broken up or traded for thirty-foot open motor boats which could take visitors out in the bay or double up as an in-shore fishing boat.

Minehead harbour was also used by visiting craft who might be chartered in for temporary local contracts or by vessels windbound and unable to continue their journeys up or down the Channel. Several notable vessels rested over at Minehead in this way. Among the regularly-chartered vessels seen was the ketch *Destiny* of Watchet, often skippered by Captain 'Griff' Pulsford, the well-known Minehead skipper and owner.

The potential of the German submarines, or U-boats, had been gravely underestimated by both sides. In the last year of peace Britain had imported 55 million tons of food and raw materials and exported 100 million tons of coal and manufactured goods. Britain's merchant fleet was the world's biggest, yet thanks to German submarines, by the end of 1916, Britain had lost 738 ocean-going vessels, accounting for more than half the required capacity to supply the country's needs. From February 1917, the German 'all-out' policy of sinking everything that floated resulted in up to five ships a day being sent to the bottom. Smaller ports such as Minehead started to lose the little coasters and colliers that were the mainstay of local trade.

It is almost unbelievable today to understand why the British government did not institute a convoy system earlier, but it took these incredible losses to spur them into doing so. True, they had made suggestions as to the route that local vessels might like to take but local skippers often felt they knew better and many proved they actually did.

Now the war had come right into the homes and cottages of the coasting seamen. Vessels and crews were lost daily and it was too much to expect that a voyage to the French coast with coal from Cardiff would be without incident. Captain Shaw, the schooner captain, told John Gilman that many of the smaller insurance companies and mutual societies faced with such losses, could no longer survive; after putting up their premiums to alarming levels, they finally gave up. Local skippers knew the risks they were running and endeavoured to keep clear of the English Channel ports if they could.

Freight costs rose, with the need for coal and grain especially taking the price for one trip to within the value of the vessel itself. The April of 1917 saw freights of between £5 and £6 per ton offered by the coal merchants of Newport and Cardiff to local schooner skippers willing to load for

Fécamp, Paimpol and other ports in northern France. France was desperate for coal at this time as all her reserves had gone; she relied entirely, as did the war machine, on those imports that managed to evade the U-boats. Tom Rawle, son of Thomas Hamson Rawle, was about fifteen when war broke out, and served as ship's boy on various vessels during the war. He told me the routine:

'We'd go across to Newport for coal and if early enough get back to Minehead so that the crew could have another night ashore with their families. We'd lie up off White Mark and go ashore in the boat. We had been told to wait at Falmouth until there was a sufficient number of vessels ready for convoy. Sometimes this could mean a wait in Falmouth which meant pulling ashore again for provisions. When it was reckoned the time to sail, our escorts, smacks and converted steam trawlers armed with four-inch guns, arrived from Plymouth and slowly the whole fleet got sail on and crept out of the river into the open sea. Everyone was "on watch" all the time and we all had "periscopitis" with very good reason. On several occasions we were only escorted as far as Cape Barfleur where French motor patrol boats took over and shouted their advice.'

'This advice was mostly to keep as close inshore as we could because of the known presence of U-boats in the vicinity. Once off the harbour entrance, the pilot and the tug would come out to us and shout out about the danger all over again, urging us to take the tow [these were sailing ships] to avoid danger. We later realised that this was a ploy to take advantage of the ramped-up towage and pilotage charges imposed on a desperate situation. After the first time, we got wise to them and if possible, took the pilot only. Even then, the pilots would ask for a greater mileage than they had achieved. Knowing that we were on good freights the Customs and dock gatemen were also on the take and demanded to be tipped.'

'The trip back was equally fraught. We were ordered by the naval authorities to rendezvous for convoy off Céaux but several skippers decided not to follow and set off on their own. Trusting the convoy escorts was a gamble. Sometimes those who stuck with the convoy were unlucky and picked off by a U-boat or were escorted too close inshore for safety. There were several instances of convoys getting lost in mist and fog and some of the vessels running ashore on the Devon coast.'

'The Germans knew all the regular tracks of the incoming and outgoing vessels and just sat there out of sight waiting for the right opportunity. Where sailing vessels were concerned, they didn't even waste a torpedo on them but surfaced and ordered the crew off before shelling the hell out them. On more than one occasion crews had no chance of getting a boat over before the first shells hit the vessel. We made several trips across with coal from Cardiff to both Normandy and Brittany and luckily got away with it but knew such luck couldn't last.'

Tom Rawle's good fortune held throughout the war, but he had a narrow escape when working on Harry Manley's schooner *Florence Muspratt* under Captain Jack Redd. This schooner had been built in 1869 in a Lincolnshire shipyard and was snapped up in in 1893 as a bargain for £500 by Robert Marley of Porlock Weir. However, she proved too deep in draught for Porlock Weir and even for Minehead, so she traded from other Channel ports with a crew including Porlock, Watchet and Minehead men such as Tom Rawle. The *Muspratt* was still in her prime as these craft were built to last. She sometimes came into Minehead where she used to lie up at the mooring post in the centre of the harbour.

The *Muspratt* seemed to have a charmed life through the early years of the war making many good passages to and from France and Ireland and across the dreaded English Channel. As the war developed and shipping losses mounted, freights rose and those who were lucky made a lot more money than was usual in the trade. However very few of the larger schooners escaped some form of trouble. On the morning of 5 September 1917, under the command of Captain Jack Redd, the *Muspratt* set sail from St Malo, bound for Newport in ballast to pick up a cargo of coal. Her orders were to rendezvous five miles north of Lezardrieux, or 'Lizzydreel' as the lads called it, where she would join up with a convoy and escort.

Six vessels converged on the little port that day, four British and two French. The convoy was small by comparison with some of the fleets that regularly gathered here. Although the Germans were very aware of the place it was still one of the regular points for assembly. All appeared to go well and the little group moved slowly off setting a course in a light breeze towards the south coast of England. Just after teatime a U-boat appeared and fired a warning shot across her bows. Immediately after this, shells began to explode in the vessel itself. Captain Redd ordered the crew to abandon ship immediately and the boat was hurriedly swung over the side on the burtons. Tom remembers how Captain Redd was anxious to save the vessel's paperwork and what valuables he could. Then the mate, Augustin Johannson, remembering something important, rushed below and was killed by a shell crashing through the side. The rest of the crew, Lewis the cook and Tom Rawle together with the captain, scrambled into the boat and cast off. Within minutes, the *Muspratt* had sunk. The boat was then ordered alongside the U-boat and the Captain instructed to give what information he could about the vessel and its destination. The Germans seemed not unfriendly and directed them to where they had sunk another vessel so they might link up with the crew. It turned out that two further vessels were sunk that afternoon in the same area, the schooner *Emma* of 73 tons and the schooner *Francis* of 89 tons.

Estimating their position to be about seven miles north of the Sept Isles and twelve to fourteen miles north of the French coast they set a course accordingly and began to pull towards the land. Fortunately it was not too cold and there was only a moderate sea running and by daybreak they could just make out the shapes of two French schooners ahead. As they drew up with them, the French hailed them offering them aid and hot coffee, but fearing that the U-boat might still be in the offing, they pulled on. They were picked up by a French patrol boat later that morning and taken into Lezardrieux. There they were given food and were taken on into neighbouring Paimpol and fitted out with warm clothing. They then returned to St Malo to await a steamer to take them back to England.

At the first opportunity Captain Redd sent the following telegram to the owner: 'To Manley. Porlock. Muspratt sunk. Mate killed. Rest crew safe. Redd'.

The next available cross-channel steamer arrived at Southampton on the morning of 12 September where Captain Redd and his crew entrained for Minehead. Whilst waiting on the station at Taunton he sent a further telegram to Mr Manley, announcing their arrival and their expected return home that night. There is a story told that the crew slipped off the train at Dunster and made their way along the beach to Minehead because they wished to avoid the folk who might be waiting at the station to greet them. Dressed as they were in secondhand, ill-fitting gear and having nothing saved from the disaster, it is not surprising they might wish to escape observation and get back to the safety and warmth of their homes before having to tell their story.

After his escape, Tom Rawle travelled to Bristol and joined the *Ino*, a coaster owned by the Bristol Steam Navigation Company. He survived the war, but Captain Redd was less fortunate. After this trip he took command of the *Chrystalite*, a three-masted schooner out of Swansea. With him went Jack Martin and Clement Hunt of Quay Street and another Minehead man. They were never seen again: the schooner was reported lost with all hands a few days later. Minehead also received news of the loss of the *Perriton*. One of T.K.Ridler's ships, she had been a regular trader until sold on some years before the war. She was sunk by a U-boat on 19 January 1918, twenty miles east of Berry Head.

After the war, Britain never regained her position in world trade. Her losses were too catastrophic for that. Neither did she recover financially or socially from the vast toll of both human and material wealth. The U-boats alone destroyed 4,837 merchant ships and 11,135,000 tons of shipping during the Great War. We also lost 15,313 merchant seamen and the Royal Navy lost 22,811 sailors including 6,000 more merchant seamen seconded to it in the smaller requisitioned vessels. No port escaped death, damage or sinkings but Minehead seamen played their part with duty, determination and humour. Tom Rawle's story is just one among hundreds of similar stories of the First World War.

The years immediately following the war were kind at first to the coasting fraternity as freights continued high, allowing many owners to invest in engines for their craft. But the British government soon put a stop to the lucrative contracts taking British coal to French ports. The Irish trade continued steady but as the years went by, larger motor coasters replaced the sailing vessels and only a very few of the latter managed to survive. By the end of the decade, Minehead only had one locally-owned sailing vessel still trading, the *Orestes*, which continued to trade until 1929, though other sailing ships visited from time to time. The *Orestes*, a 57-ton ketch, had been brought to Minehead by its owner T.K.Ridler, in 1896.

Many smaller vessels had been lost in the war, and by the end of the 1920s their earlier function of market runs for the coastal towns had largely been taken over by motor lorries, which now brought the groceries by road. Heavy or bulky objects destined for Minehead still travelled by rail, except for coal, which it was easier to bring across the dozen or so miles from South Wales by sea. So coal and pit props were now almost the only local maritime trade, along with bricks or cement. In the summer, when the coal trade was slack, the *Orestes* would load up with culm from Saundersfoot in South Wales and limestone from Aberthaw, and dump it by the limekilns on Quay West for firing in the winter. Or T.K.Ridler ('Tom') and his skipper, Captain Philip Stanley Rawle (later known as 'Old Stan') and the crew would take a load of bricks or coal to Ireland on the *Orestes,* picking up in return some cargo for Cornwall or the Isle of Man. They would be away for a month or so, taking their time and treating the break from carrying coal and yet more coal as a summer holiday.

Minehead had continued to offer holidays to civilians during the war; now the town began to return to normal and improve on its facilities as a seaside town. One essential feature was a promenade, so the remaining buildings opposite the *Red Lion* were demolished, with Captain Vickery's cottage the last to go. The Quay Town part of the sea wall was finally completed and by 1920 there was a pleasant Green where once there had been cottages; the Promenade could now continue all the way to the harbour. The road here was raised a few feet in an attempt to prevent flooding of the cottages on the landward side. This is why the doors of the cottages in this part of Quay Street are now below road level; however, the houses were still susceptible to flooding, so like most of the houses in the street, their doorposts have grooves so that boards can be slid in front of the door if necessary. According to a neighbour in Quay Street, residents used to keep handy a bucket of blue clay from Warren Point to seal in these boards if floods threatened. The council would later supply sandbags, but these had their own drawbacks, as they could split and block drains, making the flooding even worse. Flooding would continue to occur when a higher-than-usual tide coincided with a north-east gale until a new sea wall was built in the late 1990s.

Campbells' White Funnel steamers returned for the August Bank Holiday of 1919. Some ships had been lost in the War; those that remained had been refitted and were smart in new paint over their wartime camouflage.

The Yellow Funnel Fleet from Cardiff offered competition for a while, until they were bought out by Campbells, who acquired their two paddle steamers, renaming them *Brighton Queen* and *Brighton Belle*, as their base was in Brighton. Campbells also bought out the company which owned the pier, which had suffered severe losses during the war. The steamers continued to offer employment for many residents of Quay Town: young boys often started out on a seafaring life as deck boys, cleaning up after the passengers and sleeping on board.

Jobs available on the quay without actually going to sea included work in the harbour as riggers, loaders and unloaders. Painters and carpenters were also needed, to repair damaged vessels or brighten up weatherbeaten ones; shipmasters took a pride in their vessels. Some carpenters, such as Mr Chapman at number 11, made model boats for the thriving Quay-Town model boat club or their own satisfaction. And of course there was always fishing to do, to feed one's family or to sell on the quayside or both, especially in the off-season.

Seamen and fishermen usually wore blue serge trousers and a distinctive knitted seaman's jersey, usually topped off with a flat cap. The trousers would be tucked into knee-length leather boots, kept waterproof with plenty of dubbin. The life jackets of those days were bulky affairs made of kapok, which became heavy when sodden; some seamen, such as Frank Rawle, preferred not to wear them; they just took extra care. And yet, unlike Frank, many seamen did not know how to swim.

Inshore fishing was usually by means of nets or a longline, though one could of course just fish off the quay or over the side of a boat with a handline, as leisure fishermen do today. The commercial fishing fleets had vanished before the War; those former fishermen who could afford it had switched to 30-foot open-decked motor boats to take visitors round the bay. But small-scale fishing continued; sea bass, mackerel and conger eels were taken; occasionally there would be a freak shoal of herring, such as once when Frank Rawle and his father Tom Hamson Rawle took in so many fish they just shook the nets into the boat and returned to the harbour with their catch, leaving the nets set. When they went back for the nets, these too were full of fish. But such shoals were now rare. Even so, an experienced fisherman who knew where to set his nets could, if he beat the other boats back to the quay, make a profit from being the first to sell his catch to the fishmongers and members of the public.

The fishing boats would leave the harbour on the ebb tide and go westwards to their carefully-chosen positions. Once the net was over the side, it would be tethered to the boat on a long line with a small flag on a pole at the far end. On the stern of the boat, a small sail kept it from running onto the net. When the tide turned they would drift back for six hours on the flood tide. The fish were packed into large round baskets for unloading at the quay. Family members would meet the boats with two-wheeled carts in which to take the catch home.

The nets used were 100-feet long and 10-foot or so deep, with meshes about an inch square. They were fastened at the top onto a thick rope, with oval cork floats at intervals. At the foot of each net to weigh it down were beach pebbles, chipped to shape with a hammer so that they could not slide out, and fastened by a short length of twisted line called a snood. The nets were soaked in linseed oil to preserve them; this made them so heavy they were taken down to the boats in a handcart. Once loaded in the boat, the lengths could be joined together with a sheetbend knot. On returning to the shore, the nets would be mended, and dried on the beach pebbles or in a net-store built onto the back of the house at first-storey level: these open-sided sheds would sometimes run along several houses and be shared by neighbours, as at numbers 45-49 Quay Street. The mending was done with a special netting needle. Captain Thomas Rawle used to mend his nets on the Green in front of his house, strung between two posts.

Another method of catching fish was using longlines known as 'spillers' in Quay Town. Fishermen used both methods, but with longlines you could go out on your own. The lines consisted of several hundred metres of stout fishing cord, baited at armspan intervals with worms or sprats on hooks suspended on 18" snoods. At each end of the line was a float with a weight under it. The fisherman would place the baited line on the gunwale, toss out the first float and weight and quickly row or motor forward. The rest of the line would fall overboard as you went along, and the last weight was thrown in at the end of the line. Then it was simply a matter of waiting three to four hours before pulling in your line and taking off your catch.

Leisure-time hobbies in Quay Town included model-sailboat racing (with boats as big as four feet long) and pigeon-racing, especially as the century wore on. The tradition of the Hobby Horse was also enthusiastically kept up. Besides its accustomed route through the town on Mayday, the Quay Town Horse used to go and dance in front of what is now the *Hobby Horse Inn* for the amusement of visitors and the benefit of Quay Town. One year some visitors were unkind enough to first heat up the pennies they threw to the collectors; this apparently caused much amusement to everyone except those with burnt fingers.

The *Red Lion* (now the *Quay Inn*) was one of the hotels listed in various Minehead guides as suitable for visiting families. From 1918 to 1936, when ill health forced him to retire from the district, the landlord was John Etherden, who came here after an exciting career in sailing ships with the Royal Navy. He was soon an active resident of Quay Town, a District Councillor for about fourteen years from 1919, and Chairman of the Council in 1935–6. A trained firefighter, he persuaded the Minehead

Fire Brigade, of which he became Chief Officer, to upgrade their horse-drawn machine to a motor-driven one. He was also on the lifeboat committee, the regatta committee and played an active role in various other organisations such as the RAOB Lodge. No wonder he is remembered as having enhanced the social life of Quay Town.

Towards the end of the Twenties the coastal trade faded away, leaving the import of coal for the gas works, for which T.K.Ridler had the contract, almost the only trade, especially as lime was no longer burnt in the Quay West lime kilns. Fewer customs officers and coastguards were now needed: Thomas John Bull, Frank Rawle's father-in-law, was the only coastguard to be retained. The Coastguard Cottages were being sold by the Admiralty, so the Luttrells built him a new house, number 14, to the left of what is now the beginning of the Zigzag Path. Mr Bull died before he could live there, but the Luttrells allowed his widow and her family to rent it anyway.

In 1930, T.K.Ridler reluctantly sold the *Orestes*, as it was no longer fit to fulfil his contract with the gas works. To replace the *Orestes*, Philip Stanley Rawle ('Old Stan') bought a ketch in Appledore in May 1931. His brothers Bill and Tom bought a third share each in this 72-ton sailing ketch, well-remembered by Minehead folk as the last sailing vessel owned and based in Minehead: it was the *Emma Louise*, named after the wife and daughter of its first master and major shareholder, Francis Drake of Braunton. 75 feet long with a beam of 19 feet, and built of elm and oak in Barnstaple by William Westacott in 1883, the *Emma Louise* would continue to supply the gas works until its closure in the 1950s, when natural gas replaced that made from coke. When Bill left Minehead to avoid an unwelcome marriage proposal, his father Thomas Hamson Rawle bought his third share, and Bill's place as able seaman was taken by his younger brother Frank for the rest of the *Emma Louise's* trading life.

Meanwhile during the twenties and thirties Minehead continued to grow as a seaside resort, in spite of the Depression, as those who did have jobs saw their incomes and living standards rise. A week's holiday by the sea was now within the reach of most lower-paid workers. Legislation was enacted during the 1930s enshrining workers' rights to paid holidays; Minehead was one of the many English seaside towns that saw a huge increase in visitors as a result. A 1920s guide book advised intending visitors to book ahead during the summer months or 'disappointment may result'. Minehead's delightful situation and proximity to Exmoor and the Quantock hills attracted a new kind of visitor, thanks to a new vogue for hiking and cycling. But the town was also being promoted as a winter resort for those with chest complaints, who might profit from the balmy climate.

Whether arriving for a summer holiday or just on a day trip, visitors mainly arrived by train. The Great Western company was forced to extend the station buildings and platform canopy and add an extra siding to cope with the extra demand, which included luggage sent in advance as well as the usual goods for distribution around the town and beyond by cart or lorry. Numbers reached a peak in the 1930s and on some summer Saturdays Minehead was forced to become an 'open station', with tickets to the terminus being collected on the trains once they had left Dunster station.

To cater for the holiday crowds, numerous entertainments were on offer: the Jubilee Gardens, with its bandstand, was opened on 'The Green Spot' on the sea front in 1935; the Regal cinema had already opened its doors in 1934; pierrots performed on a covered stage near the present fish-and-chip shop, and various bands, including Evelyn Hardy and her Ladies' Band, performed regularly; well-known artistes were attracted to the Queen's Theatre. Best of all, for residents as well as visitors, the sadly-missed Lido swimming pool was built on the sea front in 1936. There was a row of beach huts owned by local families at the top of the beach, in front of where Butlins now stands. This land belonged to the Luttrells, and they owned a uniquely double-sized hut at the Minehead end. Wealthy folk continued to come for the season, as the annual polo matches had resumed, attracting many famous figures including the Maharajahs of Jodhpur and Jaipur. The maharajahs stayed at the castle; riders were put up at the Metropole Hotel, and their sari-clad ladies were an attraction in themselves as they took their evening stroll along the beach.

Although picturesque Quay Street was still part of the attraction of a Minehead holiday, by the end of the 1920s fewer Quay Town residents were offering what were grandly called 'apartments'; these would be taken for their holidays by lower middle-class families who bought their own food supplies, to be cooked by the landlady. Perhaps such visitors now stayed at the numerous and more comfortable houses in town now offering lodgings. (The upper middle classes rented comfortable villas in the Parks, or stayed in hotels.) The increasing popularity of the motor car also meant many visitors needed a garage and only stayed one or two nights. But an income could still be earnt from taking visitors for a trip round the bay in your rowing boat, as Frank Rawle did in the *Margret,* or for a fishing trip. Rowing boats could be hired by the day or the week. The local fishing boats by now all had motors, though they were still fitted with sails in order to save fuel when possible.

Fishing seems to have been a major attraction for visitors, mentioned prominently in all the guide books. Ward Locke's *Red Guide*, for instance, noted that 'arrangements can always be made with any of the Old Salts [who were obviously part of the attraction] living near [sic] for a day's sea-fishing, conger, whiting, thornback [a kind of skate], cod and other fish being among the possible takes'. The later revised version of this guide (1939) refers to the Old Salts more respectfully as 'old fishermen'.

Campbells' steamers still called at the pier but the number of visitors they carried had reduced considerably from the huge crowds of early in the century. The visitors could be rowdy and even drunk; young women such as Frank Rawle's future wife Dorothy took care not to go out when the steamers were coming in; nor was it wise for them to venture out alone after dark for fear of drunken seamen. The buses waiting at the Quay to take passengers from the steamers into town and beyond were all motorised by 1927. Buses would continue to use the Quay as their traditional starting point for out-of-town destinations until the Fifties.

With the decline in coastal trade, the sailing vessels that used to crowd Minehead harbour had mostly been sold down the Channel to Braunton and Appledore, the last stronghold of coastal sail in the West Country. At the outbreak of war there was only one such vessel remaining at Minehead, the ketch 'Emma Louise', belonging to and crewed by Captain Stan Rawle and his brothers Tom and Bill (and later Frank). At this stage of her life the 'Emma Louise' still carried a full set of sails but during the war years to come, she would be fitted with a motor and begin to rely less on her sails.

Visiting sailing coasters still used the port. Captain Hugh Shaw's schooner Cambourne, his brother's Mary Jones, and the little steamer 'Wheatsheaf' made regular calls to Minehead and it was possible on rare occasions to find two or three sailing ships lying up at the quay. The harbour was now almost entirely used for leisure fishing and taking out visitors, and by Quay Town men fishing for their livelihood, especially out of season.

Earning a livelihood must have been harder than before, as there was little work available apart from fishing. Fortunately there were some large catches of herring in the twenties which benefitted everyone, including shrewd local carters who filled their vehicles with baskets and tubs of the fish to sell inland at twenty a shilling, to be salted away for the winter. One enterprising Quay Town resident, however, found a way of profiting from the carelessness of visitors to the beach. In front of the Queen's Hall there was a wooden groyne parallel with the sea front, to protect the sea wall. This, he conjectured, would trap any articles dropped and forgotten behind it, in the same way as fish were trapped in the weirs by the outgoing tide. His guess paid off, as he and his friends found items such as rings and coins. One found a gold guinea but did not know what it was, having never seen such a valuable coin before in his life.

Chapter Eight : World War Two in Minehead

The declaration of war in September 1939 brought serious concerns to everyone along the Somerset coastline. The ruthless speed of the Nazi assault on Poland had sent shock-waves through the country and the sheer efficiency of the German assault from both air and ground forces had been impressive. The first local impact was the recalling of all Reservists and as at the outset of the Great War there were a few who were snatched away almost before they had time to think about it. Those at sea, some with experience of the 1914 – 1918 conflict, found their papers waiting for them on return to their home port.

As in the Great War, many Minehead men joined the Royal Navy. Some, like Seaman Torpedoman Dennis Williams, became HO ratings, (Hostilities Only) but a few signed on for the 'Seven and Five' package: seven years with the Fleet and five years with the Reserve. They were swiftly deployed across the globe from Devonport Division (Guzz), their UK home base. Twenty years on from the last conflict, in which British shipping was very hard hit, no one wanted to see Britain involved in another battle against the U-boat.

Evacuees were installed in under-occupied houses in Quay Town. Soldiers were also billeted here. They re-established a narrow, now overgrown track which zigzagged up behind the harbour to the road to Greenaleigh: a useful short cut for them to the top of North Hill, where there was a troop-training area and later a prisoner-of-war camp.

The first six months of the war, called by some 'the phoney war', did not see the anticipated invasion by Hitler that was feared. There is no doubt that if he had decided to push across the Channel at the outset of hostilities he would have had little real opposition. We just were not ready. However those first six to eight months of the war bought us time enough to bring aircraft numbers up to strength, refit and man the fleet and start to train the manpower needed to support a growing army. Where defences were concerned, with an invasion still very much in the frame, an emergency programme of shore-based defensive projects was initiated along all the stretches of coast that might provide a foothold for assault troops. Plans for a secret 'underground army' were put in place and training established.

In the early spring of 1940, the shape of Minehead's sea front and foreshore was changed by the hasty erection of concrete pyramids topped with iron spikes on all the slipways. Hundreds of twelve-foot timber posts were driven into the sands about fifteen feet apart; several concrete blockhouses topped with shingled roofs were built, and two ex-naval four-inch guns sited on the quayside. All this I watched myself as a boy, writes John Gilman, as over several months they grew like unwieldy and incongruous art forms out of tune with their surroundings. Looking back at these defences after a gap of many years it is all too obvious that had a Nazi invasion force attacked at this point, it would have had little difficulty in rolling right over them all with ease. However, at the time it helped to mitigate the growing awareness of the grave national situation as Nazism quickly extended across Europe, leaving Britain standing alone. With the fall of France, the dreaded U-boats had access to the Western Approaches from the Atlantic ports rather than being restricted to the Baltic ports. As feared, they soon began to take a significant toll on British shipping.

The blockhouses on the front were designed to house four Bren-gun teams and their ammunition. They had an entrance at each end, and the whole block was built with a concrete-slab roof overlaid with a gabled shingle-roof elevation to disguise it. Smaller machine-gun posts were set up in pill boxes built from beach stones and topped with earth and turf. There were three in Quay Street: one opposite the old Red Lion, one opposite what is now the bottom of the Zigzag Path, and one in front of number 43. One former resident recalls that after being built, they were locked and never used even for practice. Several pill boxes still remain intact, further along the coast, not far from the railway line between Warren Point and Blue Anchor.

The posts were driven into the beach by gear mounted on the back of a lorry which was driven up and down the foreshore at low tide until it was decided there were enough to provide an adequate barrier to landing craft. On one occasion, the lorry became bogged down in soft mud and was abandoned, with its exhaust plugged, until the tide receded. It appeared again a bit the worse for wear but was soon in operation again. The teams that put up the pill boxes had them up in a week, but the men grumbled about the weight of the big stones that made up the base. Local children watched fascinated as barbed wire and notices prohibited access to places they used to think of as theirs. North Hill was now designated as a troop-training area. Later the access road was partly rebuilt to allow tank transporters to climb up more easily. The Parade and the Avenue were endowed with air-raid shelters and there were circular galvanised tanks of water set up in Wellington Square and elsewhere to help fight possible fires.

Aware that Britain was mobilising, the Luftwaffe dropped tons of anti-personnel bombs and mines all along the coast and close to port and harbour installations. Warnings not to touch any unidentified objects were quickly in place, posted outside the Market Hall and elsewhere, telling people not to touch or pick up any such objects. Children did of course but luckily the interesting souvenirs they collected were inert.

The Home Guard used to march up and down Quay Street, and at the far end of Culvercliffe, used at a rubbish tip since the Thirties, they practised firing their weapons. After they had gone home, the local lads used to go and collect the bullet heads from the earth bank, remembers John Rawle. Fitted back into the empty cartridge cases lying around, and given a bit of a polish, they were good swaps at school. It was an exciting time for young boys; the police and other authorities were too busy to pay much attention to them. John was given a 12" naval bayonet by one of the Bushen men home on leave. He wore it hanging down like a sword from a belt, another gift: 'no one turned a hair'.

After high winds, local boys used to go beach-combing, as there was always a lot of interesting debris from ships sunk in the Channel, including tins whose labels had come off. They mostly turned out to be of tinned fruit, which must have made a welcome addition to the family larder (if they got that far).

Once the guns had been placed on the Quay, soldiers were detailed to secure them and on one occasion Captain Stan Rawle was challenged at a newly-erected wooden barrier across the entrance to the Quay and told in no uncertain terms to leave immediately. Smiling, he pointed to the *Emma Louise* tied up alongside the Quay and said, 'Well, that vessel is due to sail on this tide and if I am not on board, it is not going anywhere!'

The story of the guns on the quay is perhaps typical of the confusion of the times. Guns had been ordered for several West-Country ports but because the Ministry had orders to supply four-inch guns to all merchant ships as part of the DEMS (Defensively Equipped Merchant Shipping) deal, it found itself with a shortage. Despite bringing out everything left in store from the Great War, there were still not enough; it was touch and go whether Minehead would get its guns. However when it became known that there was a faint possibility that the south-west peninsula might well become a target area as the first stage of Operation Sealion, Hitler's Invasion Plan, the guns were duly delivered.

But once in Minehead, the actual position of the guns became a problem. The ancient harbour was made up of strong retaining walls built with massive stones but infilled with rubble, topped with a roadway only intended to take horse-drawn transport and the weight of sailing-ship cargoes of up to a few hundred tons. Another factor that had to be taken into consideration was the height of the seaward-facing harbour wall, designed to take the brunt of the weather. It became obvious that the guns would have to be mounted high enough to clear this wall. Then they had to be camouflaged with covering buildings set up to blend in with the locality and render the guns invisible to aerial reconnaisance. Consequently, two quite tall buildings had to be constructed, each with shingled roofs of the same pattern as the blockhouses along the Promenade.

Now all was set to test-fire the guns. No-one on Quay Street was surprised when, on firing, huge cracks appeared in the structure of the harbour. These were quickly filled with beach stones and concrete; the gun teams were told to limit their practice to essential use only. Moreover, whilst training the guns, it was soon apparent that their position prevented them from firing down the Channel because the pier was in the way. As this was the very direction from which an invasion was expected, permission was quickly sought to demolish the pier. As 1940 drew on into summer, the pier was cut down and rendered into measured lengths to be towed on lighters across the Channel to Newport. Then, much to everyone in Quay Town's disgust, as the threat of invasion receded and the demand for four-inch guns remained high, the Ministry decided that some coastal batteries could stand down and the guns be used elsewhere. So the guns were taken away but nothing could restore the pier, still sadly missed by Minehead residents.

The wooden barriers, of course, remained, but most Quay Town inhabitants found a way to get around security on the harbour as they went about their daily lives. Fishing continued and the local boat owners still had access to their boats. The lifeboat, under the control of the Local Secretary, Mr J.S.Lawrence, was put on a war footing, with responsibility for a busy sector of the Bristol Channel. The Channel itself was an important highway. From the outset of war the convoy system had been adopted without the painful, expensive delays of the Great War. All vessels that could be pressed into armed service were taken over and as in the previous conflict, pleasure steamers were once again painted grey and deployed where needed. With the ports of Cardiff, Avonmouth and Bristol as close as they were, it was no surprise to see a crowd of vessels lying in Barry Roads or slowly steaming up towards Portishead with their escorts. Escorts had facilities at Swansea and were often sighted as they were deployed in the Channel.

One Quay Street lad found himself serving as an A/B (able seaman) on board one of the Escorts serving in the Western Approaches and based in Belfast. One autumnal evening this particular escort was proceeding up the Bristol Channel on the Devon/Somerset side when a dense fog drifted in. The skipper, newly appointed and unfamiliar with the coast, ordered the ship to drop anchor. After taking soundings and making observations of the shoreline he announced to the First Lieutenant, 'Clovelly, we're off Clovelly. We'll stay here until the weather clears.' The next morning the Minehead man overheard the First Lieutenant remark, 'Nice place, Clovelly.' 'It's not Clovelly', he said. 'You're off Porlock Weir and too close inshore. If I had permission I could walk home in ten minutes!' He was reprimanded for speaking out of turn but he was right and the ship was moved. He was perhaps a little flexible with the truth as it would have taken him all of an hour and a half to walk from the Weir to Minehead but the nub of the matter remained the same; he knew where he was and the skipper didn't.

Other stories were not so humorous. Captain Hugh Shaw of the three-masted schooner *Cambourne* had a desperate adventure early in 1940. He was sailing from Ireland back to Gloucester Docks when he saw a tanker explode a mile or so ahead of him. To his horror a second tanker blew up not far away from the first. Captain Shaw found himself having to make his way in a wooden sailing ship through a narrow gap in a sea of blazing aviation spirit. Having no room to turn around, he carried on, but barely made it through, with scorched sails.

U-boats were soon operating within the Channel and the flotsam from their victims soon made its way on shore along the coast. One mysterious vessel with no one on board was brought into Minehead. Among the piles of twisted and charred planking and other debris, a number of empty ship's lifeboats were spotted. The lifeboat brought one in but no survivors were found. Some of the local boys took home souvenirs but had to return them once the Admiralty claimed the vessel.

Probably the closest disaster to Minehead was the sinking of the tanker *Inverdargle* off Glenthorne on the 16th January 1940. This tanker was on her way from Trinidad to Avonmouth with 12,554 tons of aviation spirit. She struck a mine that had been laid by U-33 only hours before and blew up. U-33 had been on a mine-laying sortie all along the Somerset coast in an attempt to catch tankers such as the *Inverdargle* that were making up to Avonmouth out of the regular vessel tracks on the other side. Many people remember seeing the smoke and flames which rose several hundred feet in the air and were visible for miles. Despite aircraft being on the scene within the hour and naval patrols deployed to search the area, none of the forty-five crew survived; observers simply reported a blazing sea and an almost white-hot sinking wreck.

That first winter of the war was a very cold one and conditions at sea were pretty grim. Most of the escorts, like the old V and W destroyers, were not armed with anti-aircraft guns and could not elevate their main armament to cope with attacks from the air. There were reports of guns freezing into masses of solid ice and ships becoming top-heavy with the weight of ice on them. Until naval ship-building stepped up production, all convoys during that terrible first winter were escorted by inadequate ships, poorly equipped to deal with the sudden attacks from the air. Many were converted trawlers and the little corvettes, designed as escorts for coastal waters, found themselves battling out into the Atlantic serving the bigger transatlantic convoys. Philip Stanley Rawle's son, 'Young Stan', served on one of these.

Throughout the war Quay Town men were deployed to serve in widely different global situations and in all three services. They were to be found in many front-line situations and in both the Mediterranean and Russian convoys, some of the most dangerous theatres of war that could be found. However others, closer to home, also had war work to do. This area was home to a wireless-receiving station allied to the SOE (Special Operations Executive).

In the 1960s, when my family moved from Minehead to Blue Anchor, remembers John Gilman, our near neighbour was Mr J.S.G.Lawrence, the long-serving Secretary of the RNLI at Minehead from just before the war until 1965. He was awarded the RNLI's gold badge in 1966. I spent many evenings chatting with him over a glass of whisky while he cast his mind back to the war years. Besides the ship's radio in the drawing room which enabled him to keep in contact with the lifeboat when it was out on a mission, he had set up a transmitter in the attic to exchange crucial timed messages with British agents operating in occupied Europe. As my own father had been one of the team that helped to develop their miniature radios, to be concealed in suitcases, we were able to talk about his work.

Mr Lawrence, together with Mr Gerald Lysaght of Chapel Cleeve, whose Estate Manager he was, was also a key figure in the British underground movement, where local-area units were made ready to resist any invasion by the Germans. Trained in sabotage, in hit-and-run raids and in the use of explosives, these intrepid local bands were intended to become the 'thorn in the side' of any occupying forces. Mr J.Dell, whose knowledge of things nautical was huge, worked closely with Mr Lawrence in all aspects of this work for the government, which involved among other things the use of carrier pigeons and the setting up of 'secure houses' for agents in transit.

Meanwhile Mr Lawrence was also on the quay daily at Minehead as secretary of the lifeboat. The decision to launch was his and he took this responsibility seriously. He could not risk the boat being unavailable should a crisis occur: the lifeboat had to be in constant readiness in case of a grave emergency. As it turned out, the lifeboat did not come to have an extensive war service even though it was crewed by men of vast experience and local knowledge. The current lifeboat had only been launched in 1939; it was the first to be motorised. The *Kate Greatorex* was built according to a new design, the 32-foot Surf Class, of which only nine were built. She was driven by the Gill jet-propulsion drive, which did away with the necessity for screws, a bonus on rocky and pebbly foreshores. She soon proved a good sea boat and was used successfully in several 'shouts' locally.

On the afternoon of 19 December 1941, Lawrence received a call from the Area Commander, Admiral Casement, reporting a sighting made from the Warren Point lookout of a partially-floating object revealed at low water just into Blue Anchor Bay from Warren Point. He was invited to investigate and report. At this time the Germans were experimenting with both acoustic and magnetic mines and it was vital that information from unexploded mines and bombs be passed on to Mine Counter Measures. But the object might just be the remains of a wreck. Mr Lawrence conferred with the lifeboat coxswain: he felt he could not justify the launch of the lifeboat. Instead, the coxswain, John Slade, offered to take his own motor boat, *Mouette,* out to have a look. John took his shore signalman, young Tom Escott, with him and together they motored across the bay towards the reported object.

As the *Mouette* nosed in alongside, there was a huge explosion that was heard right across the town. It quickly became obvious from the size of the flash observed from the shore and the massive detonation, that the object must have been a magnetic mine, probably dropped by parachute. John Rawle and his friend George Yeandle saw the explosion and a few days later they found the transom of the *Mouette* on the beach and gave it to John Slade's widow. Tom Escott's body came ashore within days but of John Slade no trace was ever found.

Two fine men, both lifeboatmen, lost their lives and were honoured at home by a plaque in the Lifeboat House and later, on the Roll of Honour in the Books of Remembrance in Westminster Abbey. They are also commemorated in St Peter's-on-the-Quay. They were the only casualties from enemy action in Minehead, as the town itself was never attacked, although there were, of course, casualties among those who had left the town to serve in the armed services. But the bombing of Cardiff and Barry just across the Channel was clearly visible from Minehead.

Meanwhile people in Quay Town went about their daily lives. Grain was still imported from Ireland and stored in the upper storey of T.K.Ridler's store. The *Emma Louise* continued to make trips across the Bristol Channel to Barry or Cardiff, transporting cement, pit props, coal for the gas works and other material. She was fitted with a motor during the war but used sail whenever possible, not only to save fuel but also to avoid setting off a mine. Athough there was a machine gun on board, none of the crew knew how to use it. The *Emma Louise* was actually strafed twice by enemy planes but fortunately sustained little damage. The vessel herself was thoroughly cleaned after unloading but Frank Rawle would come home to number 14 covered in coal dust. His wife Dorothy would throw several buckets of cold water over him before he was allowed to come into the house and finish getting clean at the kitchen sink.

John Rawle's boyhood memories of life at number 14 are probably typical of many growing up at that time in Quay Town. The house was always cold because the living/dining room was the only room to have a fire and gas lights. Gas was too expensive for everyday life so candles were used instead. There was an inside lavatory but the narrow bathroom was only just big enough for the bath, which was supplied with hot water from a gas-heated copper boiler — it cost two shillings-worth of gas to half-fill the children's weekly bath. In the kitchen, water for washing clothes and sheets was heated in a large iron basin over a fire. The wet laundry was then squeezed through a mangle and hung on lines in the large garden at the foot of the Zigzag Path. Here Frank Rawle also grew vegetables, and later John Rawle would have his pigeon loft. John's grandmother, Mrs Edith Bull, like many other women in the street, took in washing, in her case from the Mount Royal Nursing Home where her daughter Dorothy was a nurse. Mrs Bull also nursed elderly ladies and washed and laid out the dead for burial, a job far better paid than doing other people's laundry, as no one wanted to do it. At spring-cleaning time, the carpets were taken out and spread over a row of double stakes that used to stand near the sea wall opposite the shelter. The grandchildren enjoyed helping to beat out the dust with a large bamboo carpet beater.

Quay Town in the forties was like a miniature village, remembers John Rawle. All the women were called 'Auntie' by the children, who, if they got up to mischief anywhere would get a clip on the ear from the nearest adult, and often a follow-up clip at home too: 'He wouldn't have whacked you for nothing'. If they hurt themselves, Mrs Smith at number 49, a district nurse, would patch them up. Girls and boys growing up in Quay Town had the run of the beach, the harbour and the moors. They had their favourite haunts on North Hill, played cricket on the Green and fished for crabs off the low sea wall opposite numbers 35-37, using limpets as bait. John Rawle and his sister Pat were sometimes taken by their father Frank to tickle prawns in the beach fish weirs. They would stand knee-deep in the water with a net between their knees and gently feel under the stones which formed the wall of the fish trap. The prawns would fall into their nets and fill a basket for their supper.

The boys helped their fathers collect fish from the beach traps and went fishing with them (though at least one later sailor was often seasick as a boy). The 'Quay Street Sharks' considered the rubbish tip at Culvercliffe and 'The Plantation', the wild area above Frank Rawle's garden, to be their territory. The girls had their own games, playing in the grain store or collecting whortleberries on the moors to sell to Miss Bailey, who kept a shop at the top of Blenheim Road. They swung on the rails that used to be at the foot of the Zigzag Path, played ball against the blockhouse walls and even naughtily directed their pea-shooters through the slits of the gun emplacement at people climbing the Zigzag steps. Pat Rawle's only frightening memories are of the cows being driven at speed through Quay Street from Greenaleigh farm on their way to the market, and the lorries which one day rumbled noisily past number 14 on their way to set up the guns on the harbour, killing her pet tortoise in the process. (It used to cross the street every day to feast on the grass of the Green.)

Everybody in Quay Town knew everybody else, which wasn't surprising as many, perhaps the majority, of residents were related in some way or other. The Rawles, the Bushens, the Martins, the Jameses, the Slades, the Webbers and many other families were all intermarried and had family members living in Quay Town. Nearly all the men were seamen or connected to the sea in some way. The habit of nicknames continued, with 'Old Stan' and 'Young Stan' Rawle; 'Pop' Smith and his father 'Gravy Smith', so-called because after a rare trip to London to represent Quay Town at a banquet, all he could recall of the feast was the gravy. 'Sticks' or 'Peg-Leg' James was so-called because although he had lost a leg in World War One, he moved very fast on his crutches.

Other well-known characters included Alfie Webber, coxswain of the lifeboat from 1947-1956. Alfie is still warmly remembered in Minehead as he always had a good story to tell and played the drums for the Hobby Horse, with Jack Webber on accordion. He lived at Westbury Cottages, above the old lime kilns. He was in charge of the tip at Culvercliffe. In his free time he would hunt rabbits up on North Hill with his two greyhounds.

The Martin family provided three coxswains for the lifeboat in the first half of the century: William Henry Martin served for thirty years, from 1901 to 1931, when Richard Martin took over. Then John Slade was coxswain from 1939 until his tragic death in 1941. John Martin was the coxswain before Alfie Webber. In his retirement, old Captain Bill Martin used to catch conger eels; he would lay them out on the sea wall opposite number 51a, where he lived at the time. Occasionally the eels, which had been stunned when caught but not always fatally, came alive again and started writhing around, giving anyone who happened to be passing by a nasty shock.

Former sea captain Captain Smith, according to local legend, was reckoned to have been the inspiration for the seaman with the craggy bearded face on the packets of Players cigarettes. Earlier in the century Mrs Betty Bushen had also gained fame beyond Quay Town at the age of 101 when a full-length photograph of her advertised the supposedly health-giving properties of Wiveliscombe Old Ale.

Captain Thomas Hamson Rawle was a highly-respected Quay Street resident, still living at number 11a after his family had grown up (his wife Margaret had died in 1921). From the age of fourteen, he had worked on local sailing vessels. His first command had been the *Looe*; later he was skipper of the *Orestes*. At the time of the war, he was in his seventies. His grandson John remembers him as 'a dapper little man', five foot six and with a thick head of silver-grey hair. Like the other sea captains in the street, he always dressed in the same style, notably blue seaman's jacket, dark-blue serge trousers, seaman's jersey and a captain's hat, blue in winter or with a white cover in summer. For special occasions, he had a blue pin-striped suit, a waistcoat with a watch hanging from a thick gold chain, a white shirt with a stiff collar, and black polished shoes, all topped by a trilby hat. On Fridays he would make his way to the 'Buffs' (RAOB) Lodge in town, of which he was the oldest member and on the Roll of Honour, perhaps calling at Dewars Pub on his way home for a whisky (though he rarely drank otherwise) with his friends.

Captain Rawle had been persuaded to have gas in the early days of that utility, but found it too expensive. Because the gas company was tardy in cutting off his supply, he cut through the pipe with an axe just below the meter, stuffed a cork into the pipe and threw the meter into the alley, from whence it was eventually collected. The corked lead pipe was still there well into the forties. Electricity, however, was a different matter.

Captain Rawle was one of the first to have electric lights installed. He also led the way in getting a bath installed (occasionally used to store herrings, if he had a large catch), and later a telephone. 'The Old Man', as his sons called him, though not to his face, when they called him 'Cap', was the epitome of a patriarch. His family visited him frequently, especially those living in Quay Town. His sons Tom, Philip Stanley and Bill (whose place was later taken by Frank) crewed the *Emma Louise*, which took over the run to Wales for coal from the *Orestes*. Every morning Captain Rawle would raise the Union Jack on the flagpole in front of his house. The flagpole also displayed his notice offering sailing or rowing boats for hire.

As the war progressed, the United States joined the Allies and it was decided that the first priority was to be the defeat of Germany before the war in the Far East could be tackled. The spin-off for Minehead was that North Hill would become a training ground for battle tanks preparing for the Allied landings in Occupied Europe. The cost to North Hill was quite dramatic as local children found out when they tried to access one of their favourite playgrounds in and around Moor Brake.

The first barrier across the road was just up from the hairpin bend at the top of Valley Woods. A sentry was stationed at this point and there were often several soldiers on duty alongside him. It was relatively easy for the youngsters to creep around him among the gorse bushes and proceed carefully up to Moor Brake where, to the right, the tank-repair shops were situated on either side of a concrete roadway cut into the wood itself. This was always a busy place and it is hard to realise today just how many large Nissen huts there were built among the trees. The trees have recently been cut back, revealing the extent of the buildings.

Further out on the open moorland there were several concentrations of concrete bunkers, observation houses and even rail-mounted trolleys set up to carry moving targets for the tanks to fire at. Another concrete roadway descended towards the sea for about 200 yards, ending with a solid platform on which tanks could practice firing, with their shells landing in the sea. I can't believe, even now (writes John Gilman), the number of vehicles there were up there: huge six-wheeled army lorries, jeeps and command cars beside the larger articulated vehicles designed to carry individual tanks. Most of the tanks were Shermans. The other feature of the landscape, apart from bull-dozed ditches, ramps and gulleys, was the huge piles of spent ammunition, shell cases and broken military hardware littering the moors. Slit trenches were everywhere and it was easy to fall into them, as they were half hidden by the heather. Of course we were always caught and manhandled off the site with a grin but the Americans were never harsh and usually treated us with a smile and a packet or two of gum. Souvenirs were sought by almost everyone and we soon collected the small brass US lapel badges and a range of 'off-ration' sweets and chocolates. The friendliness of the Americans made all the difference in our bleak war-time lives. Food, too, was rationed: ration books were issued at what is now the former police station at the top of Blenheim Road.

Towards the end of the war, the rationing of petrol meant that some fishermen converted their motor boats to run on paraffin once the engine had warmed up. For the same reason horses were still often used to pull carts. One such was the huge drayhorse that helped Mr Meads, of 1 Blenheim Cottages, deliver parcels from the railway station. This horse met a tragic end. Startled somehow when waiting outside the police station one day, it galloped down Blenheim Road, dragging its cart behind it. John Rawle, who was on his way home from school, saw it careering down the road towards the beach. 'Despite the brake being on, the horse and cart disappeared ... leaving a trail of sparks from the iron-shod wheels ... the galloping beast tried to turn towards the railway station as it neared the sea wall'. But carried by its own momentum, the horse failed to turn and tried instead to jump the wall. Halfway over the wall, its back legs were trapped by the cart. The poor beast strangled itself in its harness and was dead before John and others reached it. After it had been cut free, the tractor used to pull the lifeboat was sent for to bring it to the harbour slipway.

Once the war began to turn in favour of the Allies, a prisoner-of-war camp was set up on North Hill, housing Italian and German prisoners in POW labour units responsible for several projects around the town. Some, mainly the Italians, worked on local farms. The prisoners were allowed to leave the camp at weekends and would often stroll along Quay Street, though the two nationalities never mixed and would even cross the street to avoid each other. Some Quay Town women such as Frank Rawle's wife Dorothy would take pity on them and offer them cups of tea as they passed by. Sometimes the prisoners would arrive with toys they had made, such as wooden marionettes, to be exchanged for a pack of five Woodbine cigarettes.

Before the hill was finally declared open again after the war, volunteer Ukrainian bomb-disposal squads spent the summer of 1946 systematically removing and defusing the hundreds of live shells and projectiles that littered the open moorland, especially in the target areas. Searches by the local boys on their familiar territory soon revealed hoards of used shells and other souvenirs.

At the end of the war, the mothers of Quay Town collected food and money from their neighbours, and gave the children a party in the long room at the Pier Hotel. Nearly everyone offered to share their butter and margarine rations. The fathers organised games afterwards on the patch of sand beyond the harbour. A second party seems to have been held in the Red Lion skittle alley, after which the children marched up to Wellington Square to meet up with the other street parties, carrying flags.

Around the town and along Quay Street, the barriers came down, the ARP defences were dismantled and the barbed wire rolled up. The posts in the bay were uprooted and the Bren-gun emplacement where the Zig-Zag Path meets Northfield Road was de-restricted and left open to the elements. Today, a house exists on the site. The blockhouses along the Promenade remained for decades. One was used as a temporary deck-chair store, but they were damp, smelly, dark and unfit for any real purpose so after being locked up for a time they were finally demolished. The usual build-up of pebbles at the harbour mouth was not cleared away during the war and by 1947 it was causing such an obstruction that the harbour had to be closed to most vessels until 1951.

Five other Quay Town men, besides John Slade and Tom Escott, lost their lives in the war: Roland and Reginald Bushen, George Gould, Marcus Jewell and Lewis Slade. Their names are recorded in flowing calligraphy in a frame outside St Peter's-on-the Quay, alongside the names of the six who gave their lives in the First World War. Those seamen fortunate enough to survive came home one by one, from India, the Far East, the Mediterranean, South Africa and a host of other bases, to find Minehead and Quay Town much the same as it was when they left. It was their lives that had changed and for some, so radically that they never really became adjusted to the lack of danger, the stimulation and the prolonged excitement that had ruled their lives for so many years.

We have to end our story of Quay Town here. The authors are very grateful to Quay Town residents past and present for sharing their memories of growing up here, and for telling us stories they have heard from their parents and grandparents. Writing about people and incidents still within living memory is fraught with difficulties. We hope you will let us know of any errors or misunderstandings, and will be very pleased to hear of any more memories or reminiscences about Quay Town and its residents past and present. Maybe there will be enough for another book? In any case, the Minehead Conservation Society is building up an archive of personal recollections for the proposed Museum of Minehead, so your valuable information will not be lost but available to future generations.

Chapter Nine: Shipshape and Bristol Fashion: a brief history of vessels using Minehead harbour

'Shipshape and Bristol fashion' was the motto adopted all along the Channel coasts and echoed in every small harbour and haven. Captains and crews were passionate about their vessels and went to great lengths to ensure they stayed as smart as they could. Coined several hundred years ago, this little phrase summed up the appearance and condition of vessels trading out of the Bristol Channel. It pointed to the pride and confidence that local seamen had in their craft, epitomised by the way Captain Philip Stanley Rawle ('Old Stan') kept his ketch 'Emma Louise' in the forties and fifties of the last century. The phrase also implies a design that had evolved to suit the demands made on the craft: the range and duration of the voyages contemplated and lastly, but certainly not least, the conditions that would be met with through the seasons.

The earliest vessels working off our shores: curraghs, knarrer and snackers

Working off the North Devon and West Somerset coast and within the huge tidal range of the Bristol Channel, the craft of the earliest era, the curraghs, were both successful and long-lasting because of their versatility, adaptability and flexibility. They could weather most storms with a yielding, flexible and lightweight hull that was easily repaired with local materials and could be beached almost anywhere, with the hull used as a roof in emergencies. They could be built quickly to any size from twelve feet to fifty feet, with beams in proportion, to carry cargoes ranging from a trio of fishermen to a flock of sheep. The larger ones stepped a mast midships and crossed a squaresail yard. If pressed, these could handle an Atlantic crossing in stages. A model of a curragh was found as part of a rich hoard at Broighter in Ireland, dating from before the birth of Christ. It was of a sailing and pulling boat some fifty feet long and square-rigged. The sea-keeping qualities of such a boat was legendary: they were capable of riding over seas that would swamp a heavier boat. They owed much to their unique design with a pronounced sheer, wide beam and the flexibility of wicker construction.

These were skin and wicker boats but when the speed and manoeuverability of the Viking long ships, built entirely of wood, was recognised, vessel construction switched to the clinker-built hull form, consisting of overlapping planks shaped fore and aft. Not all Viking ships were longships by any means and good working cargo boats emerged: smaller, beamier and more strongly built. These were called knarrer (singly, a knarr). Smaller craft were called snacker or carvar. All these vessels carried a steering oar on the right hand side of the hull. This side was called the steer-board side which quickly became starboard. The rig was simple, a large square sail, hoisted amidships on a stayed mast. Sizes varied from a knarr of some thirty-five feet to a seagoing fighting ship of seventy to eighty feet.

At the same time the Angles, Franks and Saxons with their shorter but beamier craft were emerging and local differences in design started to make their way into history. The curragh was now in decline. One of the variants, the flatner, rejected the flexibility of wicker and went for long strakes of sewn timber on a flat bottom, enabling it to work in very shallow water. If anything it was a miniature copy of the larger planked trader of the Celtic shores. It soon became the typical model of the coast from Minehead, through Watchet and on to Bridgwater.

There were, naturally, fundamental design features that remained steady throughout each era. Each vessel had its forward end (for'ard) and its after end (aft). Each had its head, looking for'ard, giving rise to such well-known phrases as 'go ahead' and 'heading for'. After length, the breadth of each vessel, known as the beam after the great beams that spread the ship's sides apart, together with the depth in hold, made up the three dimensions that governed tonnage. The design might vary as to the size of the deck area or the requirements of war, with both fore- and after-castles necessary for close fighting before the gun was brought aboard. The number and size of sails gradually evolved from the simple single-stayed mast of the trading knarr and the cog to the more sophisticated holk and carrack with up to three masts that emerged in the second half of the fifteenth century.

The vessels of the Middle Ages: cogs and holks

At around the same time, the steering oar gave way to the rudder as we know it. The earliest record we have of a stern rudder is to be found in Winchester cathedral and it probably dates back to around 1180. The rudder was not a British invention. It was developed in Friesland early in the twelfth century and quickly spread to all European craft during the rest of that century. The other marked development that appeared from this time was the triangular mizzen sail called the lateen. This reached Britain around the end of the Middle Ages and persisted until it became truncated and lost its peak, becoming a spanker, or the fore-and-aft sail on the mizzen or third mast of a three-master.

Right up to the end of the sailing era, vessels might be classed as square rigged or fore-and-aft rigged. The former referred to a rig consisting of square sails only, which might be hoisted on two or three masts at right angles to the vessel. Alternatively, a vessel might be rigged with fore-and-aft sails set in line with the vessel. These sails were carried on the forestays that supported the masts or as gaff-rigged mains'ls on all masts.

From the end of the twelfth century the larger vessels seen in and out of Minehead would be cogs and holks. These would be heavy, beamy traders, carvel-built (planks meeting side to side and not overlapping) above the water-line rather than clinker-built, and stepping one mast with a large squares'l. The fighting castles used for close range fighting were by now almost extinct, giving way to accommodation aft for the master and mate, and bunks for'ard in the forecastle (fo'c'sle) for the crew. Trading would be almost all coastal with the occasional voyage to France, Ireland or Spain. A port the size of Minehead in those days would not accommodate many such craft: the bulk of locally-owned vessels would be fishing boats. Before 1422, when a new jetty was provided at the mouth of the haven, these larger vessels would have berthed on the beach. This was common practice as after cargo had been discharged over the side, it could be picked up by cart.

With around 120 tons capacity these intrepid craft became the mainstay of trade around the British Isles. They were very strongly built. So beamy were they that they were referred to as 'round ships' and easily recognised for their bulky shape. The design remained stable for the next two hundred years and the *Leonard of Dounsterre,* referred to as making a voyage from Minehead to Bordeaux in 1418, would have looked like this. It was during this time that the ship's rig had become established on a countrywide basis. Shrouds were rattled down, meaning that rope ladders were incorporated into the backstays enabling the crew to quickly access the tops and yard crossings. Sails were fitted with detachable extensions called 'bonnets' which enabled the crew to 'shorten down' the mains'l in the event of a blow. Vertical fenders of wood protected the ship's sides from rubbing up against rough quays and the circular fighting 'top' was established above the hauled-up main yard to enable crew to fire down on a potential boarder.

Carracks and Caravels

The next significant change in ship design and profile came with the carrack and caravel. The carrack is traceable to the Mediterranean but is also found in Western Europe and was common in British waters from the mid-fifteenth century. She was believed to have been developed in Italy and during the rest of the century carracks were trading from Genoa to London and Bristol. The older types had a single mast but by around 1460 they had developed three masts, the third or mizzen mast supporting a fore-and-aft lateen sail. Around 1500, the design had become standardised and quite common in all ports with European connections. A window in King's Chapel, Cambridge shows a vessel with a deep draught, a high superstructure and three masts. She is carvel-built and is fitted with broad rubbing strakes the full length of the hull. The three-masted rig had five sails: fores'l, mains'l, lateen mizzen and two tops'ls. The three lower sails each have a bonnet. The two tops'ls are small and appear to have been set and taken in by men in the tops as the halyards, braces and sheets are seen to be led into the top.

Ever since the middle of the fourteenth century, guns had been used on board ship. At first they were small and sited in the castles or on deck so the crew could fire any available scrap at the enemy. It was supposed to be a Frenchman called Descharges from Brest who invented the gun port, in or around 1500. This innovation quickly led to the construction of a gun deck set below the main deck so that larger guns could be taken to sea. They needed to be lower down to help bring the centre of gravity lower. However as the *Mary Rose* was to discover, too many guns could lead to an unstable vessel.

Developments in Rigging

From the late fifteenth century a vessel's rig could become quite complex. The tops'ls increased in size and the top-gallant sails, or t'gan's'ls, were introduced for the first time. Here in West Somerset and North Devon they were called degannels but most westcountrymen called them t'gallons. Masts were stepped in three sections: lower mast, topmast and topgallant mast, or 't'gallant mast'. The latter two could be struck (taken up and down) making it easier to manage the rig. This was supposed to be a Dutch invention of around 1570 and as the Dutch were brilliant pioneering seamen that can be believed. Around this time the first true fore-and-aft craft were making their appearance all around Europe. They carried a fore-stays'l, a mainsail supported by a gaff and sometimes a sprit extending from the foot of the mainmast to the peak of the sail, often with a lateen mizzen rigged to an extended boom over the stern. For the small regional ports of this area, these soon became the maids of all work and individually-designed models arose with local peculiarities that lasted for centuries. For Minehead and the North Devon and Somerset coast in particular, a beamy, roomy deep-hulled vessel with a good sheer and an 'apple bow' was developed. She was rigged with a single mast and fitted with a topmast and fixed bowsprit. A fores'l was carried on the forestay and a deep mains'l was raised on a gaff. Her capacity was around thirty tons and with a cabin aft below decks and a half deck for'ard, she was able to cope with a daily passage across the Channel and the occasional trip to Bristol or Padstow to the westward. She could also adapt easily to fishing and stay out of port for a week if loaded with sufficient food and water.

Fly-boats and Pinnaces

The Dutch dominated the North Sea and the English Channel for a long time and were responsible for the design and building of many good ships which were to influence the development of all European shipping including British mercantile efforts. The next significant phase was the introduction of the fluyt or fly-boat from the town of Hoorn. She was narrower in relation to her length with straight sides and a round stern.

Whilst she retained the 'apple bow', she had a shallow draught and a flattish bottom, enabling her to beach safely without falling over. However she was not able to carry a good press of sail and so was almost always lightly rigged, enabling her to manage with a smaller crew.

The fly-boat was much copied and proved to be an economical sailer and it is this model that dominated the small harbours and havens of the west where the merchants wanted a versatile, easily managed, efficient work-horse able to sail efficiently throughout European waters. The typical fly-boat would be a three-master with the foremast and the mainmast square-rigged with main course and topsail. The mizzen mast was rigged with a lateen and she carried a squares'l under the fixed bowsprit. She had a good sheer and the profile soon established a pattern for merchant sail throughout the seventeenth century.

From this model developed the pinnace, the first advance for decades and one that saw the beginnings of the first true 'ship' rig. The technical definition of a 'ship' is a vessel with three masts, square-rigged on all three; this was to become regarded as the summit of sailing-ship design. The pinnace went a long way towards achieving this goal by limiting the number of masts to three and setting a squares'l above the lateen on the mizzen. The technical difference between a pinnace and a fluyt or fly-boat was that the pinnace carried a form of head called a beak-head and was built with a square stern. As a man-of-war she could carry twenty-four guns and was seen as the epitome of warship design at the time. It was for a pinnace that the townsfolk of Minehead petitioned when their fleet was in danger of pirates and aggressive foreigners.

The Galleon

Although 'galleon' is regularly used to denote the larger sea-going vessels of the seventeenth century, it was, and still is, a loose term denoting all the square-rigged armed merchantmen and warships of the times. They derived from the fly-boat and allowed for individual expression, regional differences and the armaments required. Such a vessel might be seen in Minehead harbour after 1616 when the depth of water at the quay head allowed. Up to a hundred-feet long with a beam of some thirty-five feet, they were rigged with up to four masts: a foremast, a mainmast and two jigger mizzens crossing lateens. Brass and bronze cannons were popular and numbers aboard could rise to fifty or so of various calibres. The last great expression of this type was undoubtedly the *Sovereign of the Seas* built in 1637 and rebuilt in 1685. She carried every sail that had been so far invented and was a lofty ship indeed.

Talking of general trends, it is usually agreed that staysails (stays'ls) were introduced from the 1660's, with the first set on the mainstay when experiencing bad weather and the other sails were furled. Later were added the main topmast stays'l and a mizzen stays'l. Finally, a fore topmast stays'l was brought in towards the end of the century, so it is possible to date vessels if, for instance, they are carrying a main topmast stays'l or all four stays'ls. Also appearing for the first time, rarely at first but becoming increasingly popular through the following century was the stunsail or stuns'l. This was a triangular sail set on an extended boom or spar rigged out on the main yard. It reached its peak of use in the middle of the nineteenth century and again can be used to date ships as it became more widely used.

By the mid-eighteenth century, large square-rigged vessels were making lengthy ocean voyages and were just too big to be a part of rural life. But Minehead seamen could sail on them, for the larger warships recruited from small ports such as Minehead; the Navy respected and desired the traditional skills established in the coastal tradition. The merchants of Bristol and Liverpool also needed crews for their growing fleets, and local seamen had to be wary of being waylaid and shipped aboard vessels that would not see a home port for years. The East Indiamen needed large crews and as a result the numbers of available seamen in local harbours could be drastically reduced, affecting the livelihood of the affected community.

Frigates and Barks

Frigates began to appear from the last quarter of the eighteenth century. These were essentially light warships designed for speed and smart handling. Of around 500 to 600 tons and carrying from twenty to fifty guns, their design became more and more efficient until they were the maid of all work for the Royal Navy for the next hundred years.

The bark was another ubiquitous type from the middle of the seventeenth century. It was a derivative of the fly-boat, with both two and three masts, and could be found in almost every port. Barks were built in Minehead. Some old paintings show the site of Thomas Manston's yard in Quay West with a vessel on the stocks. Not as grand as the pinnace or as established as the fly-boat, it was another rustic work-horse that went up and down the coast and made short sea passages with almost anything offered as cargo. Non-sailors of course, were prone to call anything that floats a ship or a bark but in the case of the bark it was a term that covered most vessels they were likely to see. From forty to ninety feet, rigged with squares'ls on two or three masts, she was often locally built and manned. This was the time just before the various rigs began to assert themselves as entities with their distinct peculiarities and attributes and before individual ports and regions began to believe that their way of doing things was superior to all others.

Nineteenth-Century Vessels: Ships, Clippers, Barques and Barquentines

By the mid-nineteenth century, dozens of vessel types had established themselves in European waters in a hierarchy of size, characteristics of masting and rigging and versatility of use. As a base measure, though not of size, there was the 'ship' which, as we have seen, had three or more masts, all square rigged. The fully-rigged ship might carry up to forty sails, as did many of the famous clippers. They were designed for deep-sea routes and too big to use Minehead harbour.

Next in size came the barque rig which could be mistaken for a ship if you failed to notice that the after- or jigger-mast was solely fore-and-aft rigged rather than square-rigged. Towards the end of the sailing ship era, large four- and five-masted barques were the most economical of the remaining sailing ships with their vast dimensions. *Potosi*, for instance, was 360 feet long with a beam of 49 feet and a 28-foot depth in hold. Her mainmast rose some 206 feet from the deck and she carried 24 squares'ls and 18 fore- and aft-sails. But nothing of this size could enter Minehead harbour. On the other hand small barque-rigged vessels could easily slip into Minehead, but by this time they preferred to visit Bristol where old photographs show them lined up by the dozen alongside the former city centre quays. The barquentine was another variant, with three masts, square-rigged on the foremast and fore-and-aft rigged on the main and mizzen masts.

Further Nineteenth-Century Developments: Brigs and Brigantines

Next came the brig. A brig was a two-masted vessel square-rigged on both the fore- and main-masts. Brigs came in many sizes and variants, with the Royal Navy using this rig on a number of classes from the late-eighteenth century onwards. The *Cruiser* class of brig-rigged sloops proved extremely popular through the turn of the century. Brigs were much in use throughout the nineteenth century and can be seen in many photographs taken in the small harbours of the West Country. They persisted because of their amazing sailing abilities, being able to stand still and even move backwards when required in narrow estuaries and approaches. The big east-coast brigs used to sail right up the London River without aid from a pilot. Minehead had a brig called the *Britannia* but she had departed before photography caught her lines.

Perhaps the last major change to the appearance of a vessel around this time was the decision to split the tops'ls into upper and lower tops'l in the interests of both handling and adapting the rig to conditions. It was much easier to run shortened-down under-lower tops'ls than to send hands aloft to brail up a big topsail. Almost all vessels adopted this change and even the schooners and smaller barques followed. It was a rare sight to see a vessel with single tops'ls after the 1870s. This is another quick way to date pictures of vessels. If the ship, barque or schooner is setting double tops'ls, then she is certainly operating in the last quarter of the nineteenth century.

Economy often converted the brig to a brigantine rig which saw the vessel reduced to square-rigged sails on the foremast and fore-and-aft rigged sails on the mainmast. Often economic considerations also saw vessels cut down in rig to save the number of crew required or to make life easier for the existing crew. Cutting down brigs to schooners and schooners to ketches was common. By this time, all shipping had been classed as either 'deep-sea' or 'coastal'. The larger vessels were crowding the busier, larger ports with their huge hinterlands and commercial links to industry. In contrast, the coastal vessels were smaller, more adaptable and capable of running into almost any port in the British Isles. Small local fleets abounded and were the vital links for all domestic and agricultural needs.

Schooners and Ketches

Seen in every local harbour was the popular schooner. The variant most widely seen was the topsail or tops'l schooner. Fore-and-aft rigged with at least two masts, the fore and the main, she crossed tops'l yards on the fore topmast. She was economical, usually fast and proved a good sea-boat. The *Perriton* was built on Minehead beach and I am sure she would be afloat today if she had not been sunk by a German U-boat in the First World War. Schooners came in several configurations with two- and three-masters all common. It was permissible to cross yards on both the fore and the mainmasts and to carry t'gan's'l yards or any number of staysail variants. Captain Hugh Shaw of the schooner *Cambourne* could be recognised at sea from a great distance by his pair of tri-sails set on the fore-upper topsail yard of his three-master. He was often in Minehead and after he retired we used to visit him for a yarn.

A century and a half ago it would have been a common sight to have seen the big schooners driving homewards under a lowering grey-black Atlantic sky, their topmasts careering dizzily against the streaming clouds. Perhaps it was the three-masted tops'l schooner *M.A.James* homeward from Labrador, her ninety feet or so of Welsh oak held in the skilled hands of one of the masters of the old school of sail, a man equally at home seven days out of St John's or entering Minehead harbour with a cross wind and a nasty short sea running.

These were the days when vessels had to be found fit to weather the worst that the North Atlantic could throw at them, when craft had to stand the stresses and strains of beating a month to windward or having the sticks blown out of them. Many became legends in their own time and were sought out by seamen for their sea-keeping qualities. Others came through gales and storms that saw even big steamers lost. Watchet and Minehead both built and traded with schooners. Minehead's *Perriton* (1881) was 72'6" by the keel, with a beam of 21 feet and a depth in hold of 10 feet. She was built on the beach by Ben Williams, a noted shipbuilder of Watchet, to the order of Thomas Kent Ridler of Minehead for his fleet of local traders. As we have seen, she was sunk by a German U-boat in 1917.

We should never forget the men who took these stout vessels to sea before the days of engines and frozen food. Often starved, freezing, ill-clad and weeks out in winter weather, they would be the first to make light of their conditions. We have met and talked with some of these amazing characters and known, at the time, that we were in the presence of real sailors. Back in the fifties of the last century John knew a seaman, then in his nineties, who had spent the greater part of his life in schooners of many nationalities. It was his hands and his eyes that impressed. The eyes carried creases that only years of open decks could give and his hands were little more than gnarled, scarred, bent fists of a dark mahogany colour, still handy enough when it came to fine work.

Captain Joe Webber, last skipper of the *Perriton* before she was sold out of Minehead in 1904, was 82 years old when he retired from the sea, and thought he was being really lazy not to continue working on board. Then there was Captain Henry (Griff) Pulsford of Minehead who went to sea at the age of sixteen in 1851. He first signed on a vessel in the Baltic trade and stayed away for a twelvemonth. By the age of twenty-two he was the master of a schooner and at twenty-five, the owner of several craft trading out of Minehead. Despite the fact that seven of his vessels were lost trading out of that port, he continued at sea until he was an old man. He died, greatly respected, in 1931 at the fine old age of 96. It was Captain Pulsford after whom the old 'gallows' crane on the harbour was named Griff's Gallows.

Such men belonged to the 'no nonsense' days when the master of a fruit schooner either pitched his skill against the weather to bring his vessel in before the bottom fell out of the market, or lost his livelihood; the days when schooner skippers in the North Atlantic beat to westward day after day in the teeth of a bitter blow with low, ragged grey clouds, driving rain and never a rest from the buffeting roar of wind and sea. Tired out, soaking wet and freezing cold, yet they kept their hands steady on the wheel and their eyes aloft and ahead.

After the schooner came the ketch, perhaps the most prolific of all rigs in the closing years of the sailing-ship era. The ketch was built in every yard and creek throughout the land and this region was no exception. She had two masts, a main and a mizzen, both hoisting fore-and-aft sails. Fully-rigged, she would present with a foresail or fore staysail and if a jib-boom was fitted, a jibsail and a flying jib. The mainmast would set a mainsail and a topsail whilst the mizzen carried a gaffed jigger or spanker. However most ketches ended up cut down just as the schooners had been, to carry only a foresail and mainsail with the minimum on the mizzen. Reduced ketches were sometimes called dandy ketches. In the last years of the ketch between the wars of the last century and for a decade or two after, these craft were often motorised, allowing the rig to be reduced even further. Even the smart *Emma Louise* of Minehead lost her jib-boom and topmast and was left with only three sails to get her out of trouble if the engine failed. Often it was only the shape of the hull that belied a ketch's true parentage.

Trading Smacks and Sloops

The smallest traditional sailing rig was the sloop-rigged vessel usually known as a smack. A smack simply denoted a small fore-and-aft vessel with a single mast divided into a lower mast and a topmast which could be lowered when necessary. She carried a gaff mainsail with perhaps a topsail above. A foresail or a jib-sail completed the rig. The trading smacks could range from small craft loading twenty to thirty tons to purpose-built vessels larger than some ketches or even schooners. Smacks could also be designed for speed, like the Revenue Cutters, with their long running bowsprit and extra sails, needed to help them out-run the smugglers rife along these coasts. The navy used such ships as fleet messengers or inshore patrol boats.

Although from the mid-eighteenth century some of these vessels were technically known as sloops, either square- or round-sterned, such as the little *Eugenie* and the *Henry,* regularly seen in Minehead harbour, the term 'smack' became common usage in a wider generic sense by the first quarter of the nineteenth century. (Older single-masted vessels like the *Industry* might cling to the more dignified description of sloop.) Many ended their days as ketches with an added after-mast, because handling the single heavy mainsail was often beyond the strength of the two seamen and the boy. Tiller steering was often replaced with the wheel for the same reason, as these big smacks could be very awkward to handle in a heavy swell.

The smack rig was a marvel in its ancestry, multiple design possibilities, its variety of form and its adaptability for a particular purpose. Smacks could be refined to become the finest seaboats imaginable. The Bristol Channel pilot cutters were legends in their own time and probably the best of all the types that emerged to weather the worst that nature could throw at them. Listening to accounts from the pilots themselves, they used to heave to and ride out the most terrific gales in complete confidence that they would be safe; they would even go to sleep and wait it out before resuming a trip. On the other hand, if you wanted speed, the trading smack *Jane and Susan* of Minehead, as we have seen, beat the record for the trip to Bristol in 1861.

The smack rig was usually locally designed. However some professional yards developed a reputation for building superb combinations of hull form and rig dimensions that squeezed extra quality out of what was basically a simple idea. Hinks of Appledore was one such and Minehead mariners preferred to have a Hinks-built boat if they could commission or find one. Once ideas like mechanical roller-reefing were invented, Appledore became famous for providing this labour- and life-saving notion.

What makes a good vessel?

Throughout history, the line of a vessel and the shape of the hull was a key factor in meeting local conditions. To marry the required beam with a smooth entry and to create a counter that would allow beaching in rough weather was an art. Seamen developed an eye for a good sea-boat and looked out for a plump belly, an adequate sheer, a fine entry and a good seat in the water. The position of the mast was a point of contention with various theories abounding, but often it was eye alone that dictated the best results. The sail plan came next and the decision whether to fit a topmast or have a fixed or running bowsprit. Some vessels, especially in the late eighteenth century, carried huge running bowsprits supporting vast fore-sails to give them extra speed.

Individual longevity was also worth considering. Some vessels could begin life in one century and continue to thrive with modifications into the next; some even passed into their third century. A life of a hundred years or so was not thought remarkable and many seamen reckoned that a good boat should last a lifetime at least. The smack *Looe*, built at Looe in Cornwall in 1787, was one such craft. She came to Minehead in 1876 and lasted until 1905 when she suffered severe straining whilst trying to get off the beach at East Quantoxhead with a full cargo of limestone. As we saw with the *Industry* in a previous chapter, during these long lives vessels would be re-masted, re-sparred and re-rigged many times, often losing their original profile. Others that might have been bought into the port's fleet received those tweaks and characteristics that were the badge of the port and acquired quite individual, or to put it in sailor's parlance, 'bastard rig'. It can, therefore, be quite unwise to jump to conclusions about a vessel's history, build and rig as she might be a good deal older than she looks.

Smacks and ketches end the long saga of vessel types that were either built in or sailed in and out of our local harbours. In the end it was size and the changing nature of seaborne commerce that dictated the presence of any particular vessel in Minehead harbour. Our generation was lucky to see the last of them and John counts himself fortunate indeed to have crossed the Bristol Channel in one as a youngster.

John Gilman remembers a trip on a Minehead Ketch

The alarm went off at five o clock in the morning and I can still remember the excitement as I scrambled into warm clothing and jogged all the way to the Quay to begin what was for me one of the most memorable days of my young life. It was the late forties of the last century and I had been promised a trip in the Minehead-owned sailing vessel *Emma Louise* across the Bristol Channel and back to fetch a cargo of coal for the gasworks.

Dawn saw us clawing our way out into the rising tide with the aid of an ancient engine whilst Tommy Rawle and his brothers Frank and Captain Stan' Rawle ('Old Stan') raised sail. Our destination was Lydney for Forest of Dean coal and the *Emma* virtually knew her way there, having been under contract to the gasworks for many years. The day was clear and bright and we were soon bowling along in a light breeze. Over the Culver Sands and past the Holmes we sailed and Tom, Frank and Stan joked as they busied themselves about the deck and took turns at steering, although the *Emma* seemed to me to be steering herself much of the time.

What was a very smart little vessel was soon to change as, after waiting our turn at Lydney, we went under the railway trucks as they hurtled tons of slack into our hold, covering everything with a heavy film of black grit. We all turned to trimming the cargo and were soon as black as the vessel. The next couple of hours were spent hosing down and scrubbing away every vestige of dirt. I discovered that Captain Rawle liked a smart, clean ship and wanted to arrive back in Minehead shipshape and everything in place. As we were waiting for the tide to take us back, he started to point out the local landmarks and currents, all familiar as his own backyard and part of the great heritage of local sailing knowledge stored away by West Somerset seamen. We finally arrived back at Minehead and secured below the crane with our cargo, which would be discharged the following day. I felt obliged to return the next day to help dig out the cargo. Frank and I and someone called Vince worked hard all day loading the iron bucket that the crane regularly bounced at us. I remember being paid two shillings an hour (10 pence in modern money) for this pleasure!

Before leaving school I and another Minehead lad, Terry Winsborough, made several more trips across the Channel from Minehead and Watchet for coal either for the gasworks at Minehead or for the Wansborough Paper Company at Watchet. The Watchet trips were with Captain Allen in the *Arran Monarch*. Looking back now I realise that I was being encouraged in a love of the sea by the very professionals whose livelihood depended on it. Captain Allen and Captain Rawle were the last of the old-time shipmasters who had learned their trade in coastal sail. Once they and the last commercial vessels had left our local harbours it was the end of an era.

Bibliography

Astell, Joan, *Around Minehead* (Alan Sutton Publishing Ltd., 1995, 2002)
Binding, Hilary & Stevens, Douglas, *Minehead, a New History* (Exmoor Press, 1977)
Binding, Hilary & Stevens, Douglas, *The Book of Minehead with Alcombe* (Halsgrove, 2000)
Coleby, Ian, *The Minehead Branch 1848-1971* (Lightmoor Press, 2011)
Field, Col. Cyril, *Mastery of the Sea, The* (London & Glasgow, 1929)
Farr, Graham, *Somerset Harbours* (London:Christopher Johnson, 1954)
Giddens, Caroline, *Minehead: a Little History* (Alcombe Books, 1980)
Gilman, John, Articles in *Exmoor Review, Mariners' Mirror, Sea Breezes, Ships Monthly, Somerset Countryman, Somerset Life* and others.
Gilman, John, *The Girl on the Beach* (Marine Arts Productions, Robin Hood's Bay, 1997)
Gilman, John, *Legacy of Smoke* (a fictional re-telling of the *Inverdargle* disaster) (Marine Arts Productions, Robin Hood's Bay, 2000)
Gilman, John, *Exmoor's Maritime Heritage* (Exmoor Books, 1999)
Hancock, Preb. F., *Minehead in the County of Somerset: a History of the Parish, the Manor and the Port* (Taunton, 1903)
Jordan, Joan, *The History of Dunster Church and Priory,* vols I and II (Halsgrove, 2007, 2009)
Lamplugh, Lois, *Minehead and Dunster* (Chichester: Phillimore & Co, 1987)
Marshall, Peter, *Mother Leakey & the Bishop* (Oxford, 2007)
Pearce, Brian, *Minehead* (Francis Frith Collection, 2006)
Savage, James, *History of the Hundred of Carhampton, in the County of Somerset* (Bristol & London, 1830)
Stevens, Douglas J., *The Story of the Minehead Harbour Guns* (Nether Halse Books, 1988)
West Somerset Archaeological & Natural History Society Newsletter 40 (Nov. 1997)
West Somerset Free Press: *Hilary Binding: Notes by the Way, passim*

Index

Numbers in italic refer to illustrations

108

The Story of Minehead's Quay Town

From earliest times Quay Town developed as a separate unit from rural Higher Town and commercial Lower Town. Quay Town, earning its living from the sea, had more in common with other seafaring communities, both on the Bristol Channel and overseas, than with Minehead's other inhabitants.

Long joined to the rest of Minehead only by a track, Quay Town's independence spanned the years. Quay Street and Quay West grew into a tightly-knit, strongly self-reliant community. Many of their houses sheltered the same families for hundreds of years.

From Curragh to Ketch is an attempt to tell the story of those families and the links with the sea which gave them their livelihood. Of course our story remains imperfect, incomplete and dependent on possibly inaccurate traditions and recollections. However, sufficient traces and memories of characters living in or connected with Quay Town, such as Robert Quirke, Alexander Leakey and his mother, Nathaniel Bullocke, Charlotte Morgan, Tom K.Ridler, Billy Martin and Thomas H.Rawle and his large family, remain to paint a vivid picture of Quay Town, its harbour and its inhabitants over the centuries.

Cottages, wharves and warehouses have come and gone but the line of the old road from the ancient haven harbour to the New Quay remains a witness to the resolute souls who experienced both prosperity and poverty. Sailing ships and shipyards, hostelries and houses have left their mark on the pages of our story. We hope this brief glimpse will inspire the reader to learn more about Minehead's fascinating history.

Many hands have contributed to this book, from long-gone historians to present friends who have lent photographs and local families who have shared their memories. We welcome you to join us as we look back on a selection of Quay Town's vibrant history.

ISBN 978-0-9549043-5-7

9 780954 904357

11a. Quay Street in 1875, photographed by James Date. Lamb Cottage is the detached white house in the centre, at the entrance to Quay Street.

11b. Quay West buildings formerly adjoining the quay photographed by James Date, 1874. All later demolished apart from the white cottage in front of the Customs House. This was used to house the rescue boat.

12. Quay Street from the beach, early 20th century. The Red Lion, rebuilt in 1902, is on the left; Captain Vickery's cottage, Beach House, is on the right with its own sea wall. The groyne in the foreground was not demolished until the new sea wall was built in the 1990s.

QUAY STREET FROM FRONT. MINEHEAD.

13a. The entrance to Quay Street with the old Red Lion with its thatched roof. The flag outside is the tricolour of the Campbells' fleet, showing steamer tickets could be bought there.

Minehead, Quay Street.

13b. The rebuilt Red Lion. The notices outside Beach House show that tickets for steamers of the Red Funnel Fleet could be bought there.

14. Minehead harbour in 1900, after most buildings on the quay were demolished. Next to the new Pier Hotel is the storehouse that would become St Peters-on-the-Quay. Photograph by Walter Groves Hole.